D1365217

LORD BYRON AS A SATIRIST IN VERSE

LORD BYRON AS A SATIRIST IN VERSE

BY

CLAUDE M. FUESS

NEW YORK

RUSSELL & RUSSELL · INC

1964

FIRST PUBLISHED IN 1912
REISSUED, 1964, BY RUSSELL & RUSSELL, INC.
BY ARRANGEMENT WITH THE ESTATE OF C. M. FUESS
L. C. CATALOG CARD NO: 64—18600

To
MY WIFE

PREFACE

THIS dissertation is an out-growth of some studies in English satire, particularly in the eighteenth century, and the book is to be regarded merely as a chapter in the history of English satiric poetry as a whole. The initial suggestion for this special phase of the broader subject came from Professor W. P. Trent, to whose wide scholarship and suggestive comment I have been throughout under great obligation. Professor A. H. Thorndike, who, with Professor Trent, read the work in manuscript, contributed valuable advice regarding its arrangement and contents; while Professor J. B. Fletcher was of much assistance in criticising the sections dealing with Byron's indebtedness to the Italian poets. My colleague, Mr. A. W. Leonard, read the first two chapters, and offered much aid in connection with their style and structure. It is a pleasure to acknowledge the stimulus given by my studies under various members of the Departments of English and Comparative Literature at Columbia University, among them the late Professor G. R. Carpenter, Professor W. A. Neilson, now at Harvard, Mr. J. E. Spingarn, and Professors Krapp, Lawrence, and Matthews.

C. M. F.

PHILLIPS ACADEMY, ANDOVER,
June 19, 1912.

CONTENTS

Italian manner adopt the exotic ottava rima. This classification is also partly chronological, for the English satires, with the exception of *The Age of Bronze* and some short epigrams, were written before 1817, and the Italian satires appeared during the eight years following that date, while Byron was in Italy and Greece.

The numerous ballads, political verses, and personal epigrams, some printed in the daily newspapers, others sent in letters to his friends, constitute another interesting group of satires, about which, however, no very satisfactory generalizations can be made. There are also lines and passages of a satiric nature in other poems, but these, casual as they are, need to be mentioned only because of their connection with ideas advanced in the genuine Verse-Satires, or because of some especial interest attaching to them.

In taking up the separate poems included in this mass of material it seems best to observe, as far as practicable, a chronological order, for by so doing, we may observe the steady growth and broadening of Byron's ability as a satirist, and trace his connection with the events of his time. However, before proceeding directly to an analysis of the poet's work and methods, it is necessary to say something of his predecessors in English satire, from many of whom he derived so much.

CHAPER II

ENGLISH SATIRE FROM DRYDEN TO BYRON

ENOUGH has been said to hint that Byron's qualities as a satirist in verse are often best to be explained by a reference to the methods and influence of those who went before him. So far as his connection with English satire is concerned, Byron was indebted in part to a widespread and somewhat conventional satiric tradition established by Pope and in part also to the special characteristics of certain individual satirists like Gifford. Unfortunately the field of English satire has been investigated carefully only to the close of the Elizabethan era; it is, therefore, imperative to present, as a working basis, a brief outline of the course of satiric verse during the century or more prior to Byron's own age. Such a summary being of value here chiefly as affording material for comparison, detailed treatment need be given only to the more conspicuous figures, particularly to those to whom it is possible Byron was under obligation.

The years between the accession of Charles II and the death of Pope saw a remarkable advance in the quantity and quality of published satiric work, in both prose and verse. For this development several causes may be assigned. As the romantic enthusiasm of the Renaissance died away or exhausted itself in fantastic extravagance and license, the new age, in reaction, became gradually more reasonable and practical. Its general tendencies were academic, introspective, and critical: literature began to analyze itself and to frame laws for its own guidance; society found amusement in laughing at its own follies and frivolities; moralists were occupied in censuring misbehaviour and in codifying maxims for the government of conduct. This \critical spirit, whenever it became destructive, naturally sought expression in satire. Party feeling, too, grew violent in dealing with the complex problems raised by the bloodless revolution of 1689 and its aftermath; moreover, most of the prominent writers of the day, gathered as they were in London, allied themselves with either Whigs or Tories and engaged vigorously in the factional warfare. In the urban and gregarious life of the age of Anne, the thinkers who sharpened their wits against one another in clubs and coffee-houses esteemed logic and good sense higher than romantic fancy. Their talk and writing dealt mainly with practical affairs, with particular features of political and social life. It is not at all surprising that this critical and practical period should have found its most satisfactory expression in satire—a literary type which is well fitted to treat of definite and concrete questions.

Before 1700 interest in English satire centres inevitably around the name of Dryden. Among his contemporaries were, of course, other satirists, some of them distinguished by originality and genius. The true political satire, used so effectively against the Parliamentarians by Cleveland (1613–1658), had been revived in the work of Denham (1615–1669) and Marvell (1621–1678). Formal satire in the manner of Juvenal and Boileau had been attempted by Oldham (1653–1683) in his *Satires against the Jesuits* (1678–9). Moreover, several new forms had been introduced: Butler (1612–1680) in *Hudibras* (1663) had created an original variety of burlesque, with unusual rhymes, grotesque similes, and quaint ideas; Cotton (1630–1687) in his *Scarronides* (1664) had transplanted the travesty from the French of Scarron; and Garth (1661–1719) had composed in the *Dispensary* (1699) our earliest classical mock-heroic. Marvell, Rochester, Sedley, Dorset, and others had written songs and ballads of a satiric character, most of them coarse and scurrilous. But the work of these men, like that of their predecessors in satire, Lodge, Donne, Hall, Marston, Guilpin, Wither, and Brome, is, as a whole, crude and inartistic, rough in metre and commonplace in style. Dryden, who took up satire at the age of fifty, after a long and thorough discipline in literary craftsmanship, avoided these faults, and polished and improved the verse-satire, preserving its vigor while lending it refinement and dignity.

Dryden's satire is distinguished by clearness, good taste, and self-control. The author was seldom in a rage, nor was he ever guilty of indiscriminate railing. Seeking to make his victims ridiculous and absurd rather than hateful, he drew them, not as monsters or unnatural villains, but as foolish or weak human beings.[1] It is significant, too, that he did not often mention his adversaries by their real names, but referred to them, for the most part, by pseudonyms, a device through which individual satire tends constantly to become typical and universal. Although he asserted that "the true end of satire is the amendment of vices by correction," he rarely, except in poems which were designedly theological, permitted a moral purpose to become obtrusive.

Deliberately putting aside the octosyllabic metre of Butler as too undignified for satire, Dryden chose what he called the "English heroic," or iambic pentameter couplet, as best suited to heroic poetry, of which he considered satire to be properly a species. This measure, already employed by Hall, Donne, and others as a medium for satire, is, as Dryden perceived, admirably suited for concise and pointed expression. Having used it successfully in his plays, he

---

[1] In the Preface to *Absalom and Achitophel*, Dryden is inclined to take pride in his fairness:—"I have but laughed at some men's follies, when I could have declaimed against their vices; and other men's virtues I have commended, as freely as I have taxed their crimes."

was already familiar with its possibilities and skilful in its management, and in his hands it became harmonious, varied, and incisive, a very different measure from the couplet as handled by even so near a contemporary as Oldham.

Excellent as Dryden's satires are, they cannot be said to have had an influence proportionate to their merit. Defoe's *True-born Englishman* (1701), probably the most popular satire between *Absalom and Achitophel* and the *Dunciad*, did undoubtedly owe much to Dryden's work; and it is also true that *MacFlecknoe* suggested the plot of the *Dunciad*. During the eighteenth century, however, Dryden's satires were not extensively imitated, chiefly because they were superseded as models by the work of Pope. Of the satirists after Pope, only Churchill seems to have preferred Dryden, and even he followed the principles of Pope in practice. Thus historically Dryden is of less importance in the history of satire than his successor and rival.

In the period between the death of Dryden and the death of Pope, satirists labored assiduously for correctness. The importance of this step can hardly be overestimated, for satire, more perhaps than any other literary type, is dependent on style for its permanency. Its subject matter is usually concerned with transitory events and specific individuals, and when the interest in these subsides, nothing but an excellent form can ensure the durability of the satire. Of this endeavor for artistic perfection in satire, Pope is the completest representative.

Pope boasted repeatedly that he had "moralized his song"; that is, that he had employed his satire for definite ethical purposes. In an invocation to Satire, he put into verse his theory of its proper use:—

"O sacred weapon! left for Truth's defence,
Sole Dread of Folly, Vice, and Insolence!

To all but Heav'n directed hands deny'd,
The Muse may give thee, but the Gods must guide;
Rev'rent I touch thee! but with honest zeal,
To rouse the Watchmen of the public Weal."[1]

The lofty tone of this address ought not, however, to obscure the fact that Pope was primarily a personal satirist, actuated too often merely by the desire to satisfy his private quarrels. His claim to being an agent for the cause of public virtue is sometimes justified in his work, but not infrequently it is but a thin pretence for veiling his underlying malice and vindictiveness. What Pope really wanted, most of all, in his satires, was to damage the reputation of his foes; and, it must be added, he generally achieved his aim.

Pope was both less scrupulous and more personal than Dryden. He appropriated Dryden's method of presenting portraits of well-known persons under type-names; but unlike Dryden, who had preserved a semblance of fairness, Pope was too often merely vituperative and savage. He seldom attained that high variety of satire which plans "to attack a man so that he feels the attack and half acknowledges its justice."[2] Unlike Dryden, too, he rarely mastered the difficult art of turning the individual objects of his scorn into representatives of a broader class. His personal sketches do not, except in a few instances like the celebrated *Atticus*, live as pictures of types.

Pope, moreover, was not always discreet enough to mask his opponents under pseudonyms. Sometimes, following a device introduced into English satire by Hall, he used an initial letter, with dashes or asterisks to fill out the name. More often he printed the name in full.[3] He had no

---

[1] *Epilogue to the Satires*, Dialogue II., 212–217.
[2] See Chesterton's *Pope and the Art of Satire*.
[3] Both methods are illustrated in a line of the *Dunciad:*—
    'My H—ley's periods, or my Blackmore's numbers."

scruples about making attacks on women, a practice not countenanced by Dryden.[1] In his satire on personal enemies he was insolent and offensive: however, he seldom gave vent to his rage, but kept cool, revised and polished every epithet, and retorted in a calm, searching dissection of character. In his methods he was unprincipled, never hesitating to make the vilest charges if they served his purposes.

In matters of form and technique Pope's art is unquestioned. He refined and condensed the couplet until it cut like a rapier. The beauty of his satire thus lies rather in small details than in general effect, in clear-cut and penetrating phrasing rather than in breadth of conception. With all this his work is marked by an air of urbanity, ease, and grace, which connects him with Horace rather than with Juvenal. His wit is constant and his irony subtle. He understood perfectly the value of compression and of symmetry.

Finally he left behind him a heritage and a tradition. With all his malice, his occasional pettiness and habitual deceit, he so transformed the verse-satire that no imitator, following his design, has been able to surpass it. The methods and the forms which he used became, for good or for evil, those of most satire in the eighteenth century. From the *Dunciad* down to the days of Byron it was Pope's influence chiefly that determined the course of English satire in verse.

Byron was fond of associating himself with Pope. He paid homage to him as a master, sustained, in theory at least, his principles of versification, defended his character, and offered him the tribute of quotation and imitation. Over and over again he repeated his belief in "the Chris-

---

[1] In the Dramatis Personæ of *Absalom and Achitophel* only two women appear, and they are spoken of in the poem in a complimentary way.

tianity of English poetry, the poetry of Pope."[1]   Only in
satire, however, did Pope's influence become noticeable in
Byron's poetry; but in satire this influence was important.

Pope's chief contemporary in formal satire in verse was
Young, whose *Love of Fame, The Universal Passion* was
finished in 1727, before the publication of the *Dunciad.*
The seven satires which this work contains comprise por-
trayals of type characters under Latin names, diversified
by allusions to living personages, the intention being to
ridicule evils in contemporary social life.   The *Epistles to
Pope* (1730), by the same author, are more serious, especially in their arraignment of Grub Street.   Young's comparatively lifeless work made seemingly no strong appeal
to Byron.   The latter never mentions him as a satirist,
although he does quote with approval some favorite passages from his work.

Lighter in tone and less rigidly formal in structure was
the poetry of a group of writers headed by Prior and Gay,
both of whom were at their best in a kind of familiar verse,
lively, bantering, and worldly in spirit.   Prior managed
with some skill the octosyllabic couplet of Butler; Gay was
successful in parody and the satiric fable.[2]   The connection
of Prior and Gay with Byron is not a close one, although
the latter quoted from them both in his *Letters*, and composed some impromptu parodies of songs from Gay's
Beggar's Opera.[3]

With Swift Byron had, perhaps, more affinity.   Swift's

---

[1] Byron particularly emphasizes the correctness and moral tone of
Pope: he is "the most perfect of our poets and the purest of our moralists" (*Letters*, v., 559); "his moral is as pure as his poetry is glorious"
(*Letters*, v., 555); "he is the only poet that never shocks" (*Letters*, v.,
560).

[2] Gay's *Alexander Pope, his safe Return from Troy* (1720) is interesting
as being one of the rare examples of the use of the English octave stanza
between *Lycidas* and *Beppo.*

[3] *Letters*, v., 252.

cleverness in discovering extraordinary rhymes undoubtedly influenced the versification of *Don Juan*,[1] and his morbid hatred of human nature and sordid views of life sometimes colored Byron's satiric mood.[2]

Much lower in the literary scale are the countless ballads and lampoons of the period which maintain the rough and ready aggressiveness of Marvell, in a style slovenly, broken, and journalistic. Events like the trial of Sacheverell and the South Sea Bubble brought out scores of ephemeral satires which it would be idle to notice here. Of these scurvy pamphleteers, three gained considerable notoriety: Tom Brown (1663–1704), Thomas D'Urfey (1653–1723), and Ned Ward (1667–1731). Defoe, in several long satires, especially in the formidable folio *Jure Divino*, shows the results of a study of Dryden, although his lines are rugged and his style is colloquial. The work of no one of these men had any visible influence on Byron, but their production illustrates the wide-spread popularity at this time of satire, even in its transitory and unliterary phases.

The latter half of the eighteenth century, comparatively poor though it is in poetry of an imaginative sort, is rich in satiric literature of every variety. Nearly every able writer of verse—even including Gray—tried his hand at satire, and the resulting product is enormous. The heroic couplet as employed by Pope was recognized as the proper measure for formal satire, and the influence of Pope appeared in the diverse forms used: the mock-heroic, the personal epistle, the critical verse-essay, and the moral or preceptive poem. At the same time no small proportion of less formal satire took the manner of

[1] In speaking of the art of rhyming to Trelawney, Byron said:—"If you are curious in these matters, look in Swift. I will send you a volume; he beats us all hollow, his rhymes are wonderful."

[2] Cf. Swift's *The Puppet Show* with Byron's *Inscription on the Monument of a Newfoundland Dog*.

Gay and Swift, in the octosyllabic couplet. The ballad and other less dignified measures still continued popular for ephemeral satire. Finally there was a body of work, including Cowper's *Task*, the satiric poems of Burns, and the early *Tales* of Crabbe, which must be regarded as, in some respects, exceptional.

Of the satirists of the school of Pope, the greater number seem to have had Dr. Johnson's conception of Satire as the son of Wit and Malice, although, like Pope, they continued to pose as the upholders of morality even when indulging in the most indiscriminate abuse.[1] They borrowed the lesser excellencies of their master, but seldom attained to his brilliance, keeping, as far as they were able, to his form and method, but lacking the genius to reanimate his style.

The mock-heroic was exceedingly popular during the fifty years following the death of Pope. The satires of one group, following *The Rape of the Lock*, contain no personal invective, and are satiric only in the sense that any parody of a serious *genre* is satiric.[2] Another class of mock-heroics, modelled particularly on the *Dunciad*, make no pretence of refraining from personal satire, and are often violently scurrilous.[3] A large number of poems imitate the title of the *Dunciad* without necessarily having any mock-heroic characteristics.[4] In the field of personal, and especially of

[1] For a contemporary characterization of the unscrupulous satirists of the period see Cowper's *Charity*, 501–532, in the passage beginning, "Most satirists are indeed a public scourge."

[2] Examples are *The Thimble* (1743) by William Hawkins (1722–1801) and the *Scribleriad* (1752) by Richard Owen Cambridge (1717–1802).

[3] *State Dunces* (1733) and *The Gymnasiad* (1738) by Paul Whitehead (1710–1744); *The Toast* (1736) by William King (1685–1763); and a succession of anonymous poems, *The Battle of the Briefs* (1752), *Patriotism* (1765), *The Battle of the Wigs* (1763), *The Triumph of Dulness* (1781), *The Rape of the Faro-Bank* (1797), and *The Battle of the Bards* (1799).

[4] The most important is Churchill's *Rosciad* (1761), with the numerous replies which it elicited: the *Churchilliad* (1761), the *Smithfield Rosciad*

political, satire, are many poems not corresponding exactly to any of the above mentioned types.[1] The bitter party feeling aroused by the rise to power of Lord Bute and by the resulting protests of Wilkes in the *North Briton* was the occasion of many broadsides during the decade between 1760 and 1770.[2]

Several satires of the period, based particularly on Pope's satiric epistles, seem to maintain a more elevated tone, although they also are frequently intemperate in their personalities.[3] An excellent example is the very severe *Epistle to Curio* by Akenside, praised for its literary merits by Macaulay.[4] A small, but rather important class of satires is made up of criticisms of literature or literary men in the manner of either the *Essay on Criticism* or the *Dun-*

(1761), the *Anti-Rosciad* (1761), by Thomas Morell (1703–1784), and *The Rosciad of Covent Garden* (1761) by H. J. Pye (1745–1813). Among other satires of the same class may be mentioned the *Smartiad* (1752) by Dr. John Hill (1710–1775), with its answer, the severe and effective *Hilliad* (1752) by Christopher Smart (1722–1771); the *Meretriciad* (1764) by Arthur Murphy (1727–1806); the *Consuliad* (1770), a fragment by Chatterton; the *Diaboliad* (1777), with its sequel, the *Diabolady* (1777) by William Combe (1741–1823); and finally the *Criticisms on the Rolliad*, Gifford's *Baviad* and *Mæviad*, the *Simpliciad*, and the *Alexandriad* (1805).

[1] *The Scandalizade* (1750); *The Pasquinade* (1752) by William Kenrick (1725–1779); *The Quackade* (1752); *The Booksellers* (1766); *The Art of Rising in the Church* (1763) by James Scott (1733–1814); *The Senators* (1772); and *The Tribunal* (1787).

[2] A few typical controversial satires of this decade are: *The Race* (1762) by Cuthbert Shaw (1739–1771); *The Tower* (1763); the *Demagogue* (1764) by William Falconer (1732–1769); *The Scourge* (1765); and *The Politician* (1766) by E. B. Greene (1727–1788).

[3] Some characteristic examples are the *Epistle to Cornbury* (1745) by Earl Nugent (1702–1788); the *Epistle to William Chambers* (1773) and the *Epistle to Dr. Shebbeare* (1777) by William Mason (1724–1797); and the *Epistle to Dr. Randolph* (1796), as well as numerous other epistles, by T. J. Mathias.

[4] See Macaulay's *Essay on Horace Walpole*, page 35.

*ciad.*¹ Still another group deal, like Young's *Love of Fame,*
with the foibles and fads of society, using type figures and
avoiding specific references.² It is necessary, finally, to
include under satire many of the didactic and philosophic
poems which seemed to infect the century.³ These Ethic
Epistles, as they are styled in Bell's *Fugitive Pieces,* are often
little more than verse sermons. Obviously many poems
of this nature hardly come within the scope of true satire.
Goldsmith's *Deserted Village* (1770), for instance, has some
satirical elements; yet it is, properly speaking, meditative
and descriptive verse. The same may be said, perhaps, of
the so-called satires of Cowper.

   The body of work thus cursorily reviewed shows a wide
diversity of subject-matter combined with a consistent and
monotonous uniformity of style. In most of the material
we find the same regular versification, the same stock epithets, and the same lack of distinctive qualities; indeed,
were the respective writers unknown, it would be a difficult
task to distinguish between the verse of two such satirists
as James Scott and Soame Jenyns. During the fifty years
between the death of Pope and the appearance of Gifford's

   ¹ *An Essay on the Different Styles of Poetry* (1713) by Thomas Parnell
(1679–1718); *The Danger of Writing Verse* (1741) by William Whitehead
(1715–1785); *A Prospect of Poetry* (1733); *The Perils of Poetry* (1766);
and *The Wreath of Fashion* (1780) by Richard Tickell (1751–1793).
   ² The anonymous *Manners of the Age* (1733); *Manners* (1738) by Paul
Whitehead; *The Man of Taste* (1733) by James Bramston (1694–1744);
the *Modern Fine Gentleman* (1746) and the *Modern Fine Lady* (1750) by
Soame Jenyns (1703–1787); *Fashion* (1748) by Joseph Warton (1722–
1800); and *Newmarket* (1751) by Thomas Warton (1728–1790).
   ³ Examples are the *Essay on Reason* (1733) by Walter Harte (1709–
1774); the *Vanity of Human Enjoyments* (1749) by James Cawthorn
(1718–1761), the most slavish of all Pope's imitators; *Honour* (1737)
by John Brown; *Advice* and *Reproof* (1747) by Smollett; *Of Retired and
Active Life* (1735) by William Helmoth (1710–1799); *Ridicule* (1743) by
William Whitehead; *Taste* (1753) by John Armstrong (1709–1779);
An Essay on Conversation (1748) by Benjamin Stillingfleet (1702–1771).

Baviad (1794) only four names stand out above the rest as important in the history of English satire in verse: Johnson, Churchill, Cowper, and Crabbe.

Of these writers, Johnson contributed but little to the mass of English satire. His *London* (1738) and *The Vanity of Human Wishes* (1749) are imitations of Juvenal, characterized by stateliness, dignity, melancholy, and sonorous rhetoric, but with only a slight element of personal attack. The latter poem received high praise from Byron. [1]

Churchill and Byron, who have often been compared because of their quarrels with the reviewers and their denunciation of a conservative and reactionary government, were much alike in their arrogant independence, their fiery intensity, and their passionate liberalism. Churchill, however, unlike Byron, was always a satirist, and undertook no other species of poetry. In many respects he resembled Oldham, whose career, like his, was short and tumultuous, and whose wit, like his, usually shone "through the harsh cadence of a rugged line."

All Churchill's work is marked by vigor, effrontery, and earnestness, and the ferocity and vindictiveness of much of it give force to Gosse's description of the author as "a very Caligula among men of letters." However, although he was responsible for two of the most venomous literary assaults in English—that on Hogarth in the *Epistle to William Hogarth* (1763) and that on Lord Sandwich in *The Candidate* (1764)—he did not stab from behind or resort to underhand methods. Despite his obvious crudities, he is the most powerful figure in English satire between Pope and Byron.

Churchill employed two measures: the heroic couplet, in the *Rosciad* (1761) and several succeeding poems; and the octosyllabic couplet, in *The Ghost* (1763) and *The Duellist* (1764). His versification is seldom polished, but his lines

[1] *Letters*, v., 162.

have, at times, something of the robustness and impetuous disregard of regularity which lend strength to Dryden's couplets.   It was to Churchill that Byron attributed in part what he was pleased to term the "absurd and systematic depreciation of Pope,"[1] which, in his opinion, had been developing steadily towards the end of the eighteenth century.   Churchill frankly acknowledged his preference of Dryden over Pope,[2] a partiality which he shared with Voltaire and Dr. Johnson.   The fact is, however, that, despite his failure to attain smoothness and artistic finish, he owed more to Pope than he realized or cared to admit.[3]

With Cowper, Byron had temperamentally little in common; yet Cowper is interesting, if only for the reason that he proves, by contrast with Churchill, the range in manner of which the classical satire is capable.   He was most successful in a kind of mildly moral reproof, which has often ease, humor, and apt sententiousness, although it rarely possesses energy enough to make it effective as satire. Cowper's familiar verse, often satirical in tone, is almost wholly admirable, the best of its kind between Prior and Praed.

The satire of Crabbe is essentially realistic.   It portrays things as they are, dwelling on each sordid detail and sweeping away all the illusions of romance.   In *The Village* (1783), for instance, Crabbe describes life as he found it among the lower classes in a Suffolk coast town—a life barren, humdrum, and dismal: thus the poem is an antidote, possibly intentional, to the idyllic and sentimental picture drawn by Goldsmith in *The Deserted Village*.   The ethical

---

[1] *Letters*, iv., 485.   [2] See *An Apology*, 376–387.

[3] In his *Letters*, Byron refers once to Churchill's *Times* (*Letters*, ii., 148).   His *Churchill's Grave* (1816), a parody of Wordsworth's style, contains a reference to Churchill as "him who blazed the comet of a season."   Otherwise Churchill's actual influence on Byron was not great.

element is always present in Crabbe's work, and thus he preserves the didacticism of Pope and Cawthorn; but his homely phraseology, his sombre portraiture, and his pitiless psychological analysis of character connect him with a novelist like Hardy. Possibly some of the realism of *Don Juan* may be traced to the example of Crabbe, for whom Byron had both respect and affection. [1]

Aside from that exercised by the work and heritage of Pope, the most definite influence upon Byron's satiric verse came from the satires of William Gifford (1756–1826), which had appeared some years before Byron began to write. Gifford, who early became the young lord's model and counsellor, and who later revised and corrected his poetry, continued to the end to be one of the few literary friends to whom Byron referred consistently with deference. [2]

Gifford's reputation was established by the publication of two short satires, the *Baviad* (1794) and the *Mæviad* (1795), printed together in 1797. The *Baviad* is an imitation of the first satire of Persius, in the form of a dialogue between the poet and his friend; the *Mæviad* paraphrases Horace's tenth satire of the first book. Both are devoted primarily to deserved, but often unnecessarily harsh, criticism of some contemporary fads in literature, particularly of the "effusions" of the so-called Della Cruscan School. [3]

[1] Byron praised Crabbe in *English Bards* as "Nature's sternest painter, but her best." In a letter to Moore, February 2, 1818, he termed Crabbe and Rogers "the fathers of present Poesy," and in his *Reply to Blackwood's* (1819) he said publicly: "We are all wrong except Crabbe, Rogers, and Campbell." Crabbe, whom Horace Smith called "Pope in worsted stockings," seemed, to Byron, to represent devotion to Pope.

[2] Byron said of Gifford in 1824: "I have always considered him as my literary father, and myself as his 'prodigal son'" (*Letters*, vi., 329).

[3] The movement represented by this clique, *Gli Oziosi*, originated in Florence with a coterie of dilettanti, among whom were Robert Merry

Gifford was a Tory in a period when the unexpected excesses of the French revolutionists were causing all Tories, and even the more conservative Whigs, to take a stand against innovation, eccentricity, and individualism in any form. Since the Della Cruscans were nearly all liberals,[1] it was natural that Gifford should be enthusiastic in his project of ridiculing the "metromania" for which they were responsible.   Thus his satires are protests against license, defending the conventional canons of taste and reasserting the desirability of law and order in literature.

Undoubtedly Gifford performed a certain service to the cause of letters by condemning, in a common-sense fashion, the silly sentimentality of the Della Cruscans.[2]   Unfortunately it was almost impossible for him to compose satire without being scurrilous.   Although he may have possessed the virtue of sincerity with which Courthope credits him, he invariably picked for his victims men who were too feeble to reply effectually.   Still the satires, appearing so opportunely, made Gifford both famous and feared.   The *Baviad* and the *Mæviad* were placed, without pronounced dissent, beside the *Dunciad*.   Mathias said of the author, in all seriousness: "He is the most correct poetical writer I

(1755–1799), Mrs. Piozzi (1741–1831), Bertie Greathead (1759–1826), and William Parsons (fl. 1785–1807).   They published two small volumes, *The Arno Miscellany* (1784) and *The Florence Miscellany* (1785), both marred by affectation, obscurity, tawdry ornamentation, and frantic efforts at sublimity.   The printing of Merry's *Adieu and Recall to Love* started a new series of sentimental verses, in the writing of which other scribblers took part: Hannah Cowley (1743–1809), Perdita Robinson (1752–1800), and Thomas Vaughan (fl. 1772–1820).   Their combined contributions were gathered in Bell's *British Album* (1789).

[1] Merry had written a *Wreath of Liberty* (1790) in praise of revolutionary principles.

[2] Scott said of Gifford: "He squashed at one blow a set of humbugs who might have humbugged the world long enough."   *New Morality* has a reference to "the hand which brushed a swarm of fools away."   Byron inserted a similar passage in *English Bards*, 741–744.

have read since the days of Pope." Even Byron, so immeas-
urably Gifford's superior in most respects, was dominated
so far as to term him "the last of the wholesome satirists"[1]
and to refer to him as a "Bard in virtue strong."[2]

The plain truth is that Gifford is not always correct, seldom wholesome, and never great. Something of his style
at the worst may be obtained from a single line,

"Yet not content, like horse-leeches they come,"

of which even the careless Churchill would have been
ashamed. Gifford wanted good-breeding, and he had no
geniality; his irascible nature made him intolerant and
unjust. Moreover he lacked a sense of discrimination and
proportion; he used a sledge-hammer constantly, often
when a lighter weapon would have served his purpose. In
him the artistic satire of Pope seems to have degenerated
into clumsy and crude abuse.

Carrying to excess a practice probably begun by Pope,
with the advice of Swift, Gifford had accompanied his
satires with copious and diffuse notes, sometimes affixing
a page or more of prose comment to a single line of verse.[3]
Mathias, whose *Pursuits of Literature* was, according to
De Quincey, the most popular book of its day, so exaggerated this fashion that it is often a question in his work to
decide which is meant for an adjunct to the other—verse
or prose annotation.

Thomas James Mathias (1754–1835), like Gifford, a Tory,
with a bigoted aversion to anything new or strange, and
a firm belief in the infallibility of established institutions,

---

[1] *Letters*, iv., 485.   [2] *English Bards*, 701.

[3] Moore speaks sarcastically of this custom in the Preface to *Corruption* and *Intolerance* (1808): "The practice which has been lately introduced into literature, of writing very long notes upon very indifferent
verses, appears to me a very happy invention, as it supplies us with a
mode of turning dull poetry to account."

published Dialogue I of the *Pursuits of Literature* in May,
1794, Dialogues II and III in June, 1796, and Dialogue IV
in 1797. In his theory of satire he insisted on three essen-
tials: notes, and full ones; anonymity in the satirist; and a
personal application for the attack. His chosen field included "faults, vices, or follies, which are destructive of
society, of government, of good manners, or of good literature." Mathias is pedantic, ostentatious in airing his
information, and indefatigable in tracking down revolutionary ideas. His chief work is a curiosity, discursive,
disorderly, and incoherent, with a versification that is lifeless and unmelodious.[1]

With the work of Mathias, this cursory summary of the
strictly formal satire in the eighteenth century comes to a
natural resting-place. Only a year or two after the *Pursuits of Literature*, the *Anti-Jacobin* began, and in its pages
we find a more modern spirit. It is now necessary, revert-
ing to an earlier period, to trace the progress of satire along
other less formal lines, and to deal with some anomalous
poems, which, although satiric in tone, are difficult to
classify according to any logical system.

The satiric fable had a considerable vogue throughout the
century, and collections appeared at frequent intervals.[2]
Nearly all have allegorical elements and contain little direct
satire, their main object being to point out and ridicule the
weaknesses and follies of human nature. The octosyllabic

---

[1] Byron said of the *Pursuits of Literature*: "It is notoriously, as far
as the poetry goes, the worst written of its kind; the World has long
been of but one opinion, viz., that it's [sic] sole merit lies in the notes,
which are indisputably excellent" *(Letters*, ii., 4).

[2] Examples are the *Fables of Æsop* (1692) of Roger L'Estrange (1616–
1704); *Æsop at Court, or Select Fables* (1702) by Thomas Yalden (1671–
1736); *Æsop's Fables* (1722) by Samuel Croxall (1680–1752); *Fables*
(1744) by Edward Moore (1711–1757); and collections by Nathaniel
Cotton (1707–1788) and William Wilkie (1721–1772).

couplet, the favorite measure for fables, was also a popular
verse form in familiar epistles and humorous tales, modelled
on the work of Prior, Gay, and Swift.[1] Ephemeral political
satire continued to flourish in rough and indecorous street-
ballads, sometimes rising almost into literature in the productions of men like Charles Hanbury Williams (1708–1759)
and Caleb Whitefoord (1734–1810). With the inception of
the *Criticisms on the Rolliad*, political verse assumes a
position of distinct importance in the history of satire.

The material represented under the title *Criticisms on the
Rolliad* was published in the Whig *Morning Herald*, beginning June 28, 1784, shortly after the fall of the Fox-North
coalition and the appointment of the younger Pitt to the
office of Prime Minister. It presents extracts from a supposed epic, based on the deeds of the ancestors of John
Rolle, M. P., who had become the pet aversion of the Whigs.
The alleged verse excerpts, all of them short, are amalga-
mated by clever prose comment. The editors included a
group of young and ambitious Whig statesmen: Dr. Lawrence, later Professor of Civil Law at Oxford, who furnished
the prose sections; Joseph Richardson (1755–1803); Richard
Tickell, already mentioned as the author of *The Wreath of
Fashion;* and two former cabinet ministers, General Fitz-
patrick, the friend of Fox, and Lord John Townshend. The
object of these men was to belittle and deride the more
prominent Tories in both Houses, particularly Rolle, Pitt,
Dundas, and the Tory Bishops, by singling them out, one
by one, for ridicule. Their verse was a flippant and free
form of the heroic couplet. Although their main purpose
was political, they dealt only slightly with party princi-

[1] See the *Spleen* (1737) by Matthew Green (1696–1737); *Variety, a
Tale for Married People* (1732); and the poems of Isaac Hawkins Browne
(1705–1760), James Bramston (1694–1744), George Colman, the elder
(1732–1794), John Dalton (1709–1763), David Garrick (1717–1779),
John Duncombe (1729–1763), and many other poetasters.

ples, preferring rather to excite laughter by their personal allusions.

The marked public approbation which attended their experiment led the editors to continue their project in a series of *Probationary Odes for the Laureateship*, comprising parodies of twenty-two living poets.   The odes follow the plan of the *Pipe of Tobacco* (1734) of Isaac Hawkins Browne (1705–1760), which burlesques the poetry of Cibber, James Thomson, Swift, Young, and Ambrose Phillips.[1]   The plan of the contributors was further amplified in *Political Eclogues* and *Political Miscellanies*, which keep to the original policy of vituperation, at the same time showing a striking deterioration in the quality of the verse.   The first zest had grown languid, and in the last collection, *Extracts from the Album at Streatham* (1788), containing poems purporting to be by several ministers of state, the verse had no value as literature.

The complete product of these Whig allies is, as a rule, clever and pointed, but it is too often coarse and scandalous in content.   Although it failed in reinstating the Whigs in office, it occupies an important position in English political satire.   Despite its irregular versification and its frequently unedifying subject-matter, it contains some brilliant sketches and many witty lines.[2]

A droll and impudent, but not altogether pleasing figure of this same period was the Whig satirist, Rev. John Wolcot (1738–1819), better known by his *nom-de-guerre* of Peter Pindar, who, making it his especial function to caricature George III and his court, earned from Scott the title of "the most unsparing calumniator of his time."   George, with

[1] *Probationary Odes* also anticipate the more famous *Rejected Addresses* (1812), and the *Poetic Mirror* (1816) of James Hogg, the Ettrick Shepherd.

[2] For less reserved praise of the *Rolliad*, see Trevelyan's *Early History of Charles James Fox*, page 285.

his bourgeois habits and petty economies, made a splendid
subject, and Pindar drew him with the homely realism of
Hogarth or Gilray, pouring forth a long series of impertinent
squibs until the monarch's dangerous illness in 1788 gained
him the sympathy of the nation and roused popular feeling
against his lampooner.   Pindar also engaged in other quarrels, notably with the trio of Tory satirists, Gifford, Mathias, and Canning.[1]   His genius was that of the caricaturist,
and his vogue, like that of most caricaturists, was soon over.
However, the peculiar flavor of his verses, full as they are
sometimes of rich humor and grotesque descriptions, is still
delightful, and partly explains the merriment which greeted
his work at a time when his allusions were still fresh in
people's minds.   It may be added that Pindar shows few
traces of Pope's influence; he makes no pretence of a moral
purpose, and he seldom employs the heroic couplet.

Professor Courthope suggests that *Don Juan* owes much
in style to the satires of Pindar.   The question of a possible
indebtedness will be taken up more in detail in another
chapter; it is sufficient here to point out that Byron never
refers to Wolcot by name, and makes only one reference to
his poetry.[2]

Some of the most powerful social and political satire of the
century was written, in defence of democracy and liberalism,
by the vigorous pen of Robert Burns.[3]   His work, however,
despite the fact that it discussed many of the topics which

[1] In *A Postscript* he speaks of "the unmeaning and noisy lines of two
things called *Baviad* and *Mæviad*"; while in a note to *Out at Last, or the
Fallen Minister*, he presents a sketch of Gifford's life, accusing him of
heinous crimes, and speaking of the "awkward and obscure inversions
and verbose pomposity" of the *Baviad*. Gifford replied in the *Epistle
to Peter Pindar* (1800).   Mathias and Canning invariably treated Pindar with contempt.

[2] *Vision of Judgment*, 92.

[3] See *A Dream* (1786), a bitterly satirical address to George III, and
the *Lines Written at Stirling*, attacking the Hanoverians.

were agitating the English satirists, was not particularly influential at the time in England.

One peculiar work, significant in the evolution of satire because of its undoubted influence on a succeeding generation, was the *New Bath Guide; or Memoirs of the B—r—d Family* (1766), written by Christopher Anstey (1724–1805).[1] It consists of a series of letters, most of them in an easy anapestic measure with curious rhymes, purporting to be from different members of one family, and satirising life at the fashionable watering-place made famous only a few years before by Beau Nash. Anstey's method of using letters for the purpose of satire was followed by other authors,[2] but never, until Moore's *Two-penny Postbag* and *Fudge Family*, with complete success. Other satires of the century also employed the anapestic metre in a clever way.[3]

The Tory *Anti-Jacobin*, a weekly periodical which began on November 20, 1797, and printed its last number on July 9, 1798, appropriately closes the satire of the century, for it includes examples of most of the types of satiric verse which had been popular since the death of Pope. Founded by government journalists, possibly at Pitt's instigation, it planned to "oppose papers devoted to the cause of sedition and irreligion, to the pay and interests of France." At a critical period in English affairs, when the long struggle with France and Napoleon was just beginning and many

---

[1] Byron knew the *New Bath Guide* well, and admired it. In one of his youthful poems, an *Answer to Some Elegant Verses sent by a Friend to the Author* he uses four lines of Anstey's poem as a motto. He also quotes from it not infrequently in his letters.

[2] See *Letters from Simpson the Second to his Dear Brother in Wales* (1788) and *Groans of the Talents* (1807), both of which deliberately appropriate Anstey's scheme. Both are anonymous.

[3] See the *Epistle to my Sisters* (1734) by Thomas Lisle; *The 'Piscopade, a Panegyri-Satiri-Serio-Comical Poem* (1748) by "Porcupinus Pelagius"; and Goldsmith's three graceful satires, *Retaliation* (1774), *The Haunch of Venison* (1776), and the *Letter to Mrs. Bunbury* (1777).

Whigs were still undecided as to their allegiance, it was the purpose of the *Anti-Jacobin*, as representative of militant nationalism, to oppose foreign innovations and to uphold time-honored institutions. Each number of the paper contained several sections: an editorial, or leader; departments assigned to Finances, Lies, Misrepresentations, and Mistakes; and some pages of verse, with a prose introduction. Gifford, who had been chosen to superintend the publication, devoted himself entirely to editorial management, so that the responsibility for the verse devolved upon George Canning (1770–1827) and several assistants, among whom were Ellis, now an adherent of the Tories, and John Hookham Frere (1769–1846).

The *Anti-Jacobin*, then, planned first to revive the traditions of English patriotism and to rally public opinion to the support of king and country. As a secondary but essential element of its design, it aimed, especially in its verse, to expose the falsity and fatuity of the doctrines of Holcroft, Paine, Godwin, and other radical philosophers and economists; to ridicule and parody the work of authors of the revolutionary school, particularly of the English Lake poets and the followers of the German romanticists; and incidentally to satirise some of the social and literary follies of the age.[1] Since the verse was submitted by many contributors, its tone was not always homogeneous, and it varied from playful jocularity to stern didacticism. On the whole, however, it had a definite ethical purpose, and avowedly championed sound morality and conservative principles.

The poetry of the *Anti-Jacobin* includes illustrations of many varied satiric forms. *New Morality* is a set, formal satire in conventional couplets and balanced lines, superior

---

[1] The attitude of the *Anti-Jacobin* was almost precisely that already adopted by Gifford and Mathias; that is, it represented extreme Tory feeling, and therefore was resolutely opposed to any movement in literature which seemed new or strange.

in technique to the best work of Gifford and Mathias, and not unworthy of comparison with many of the satires of Pope. *Acme and Septimius, or the Happy Union* is a short informal verse tale, reminiscent in manner of the unedifying personalities in the *Rolliad*. There are satiric imitations of Horace and Catullus. There are parodies of many sorts: the *Needy Knife Grinder*, an artistic parody of Southey's sapphics; the *Loves of the Triangles*, a burlesque of Darwin's *Loves of the Plants;* the *Progress of Man*, ridiculing the tedious didacticism of Payne Knight; and *Chevy Chace*, a parody of the romantic ballad. Hudibrastic couplets are used in *A Consolatory Address to his Gunboats, by Citizen Muskein;* anapests, in the *Translation of a Letter*, in the style of Anstey; and doggerel, in the *Elegy on the Death of Jean Bon André*. The material of the satire comprehends events in politics, in literature, in philosophy, and, to some extent, in society. Thus, in small compass, the poetry of the *Anti-Jacobin* offers a fruitful field for study.

In more than one respect, too, it furnished suggestions for the nineteenth century. *Ballynahinch* and the *Translation of a Letter* may have had some influence on the manner and versification of Moore and Byron. Certain of the *Odes*, notably the imitation of Horace, III,25, have the delicate touch which was to mark the lighter satire of the Smiths and Praed, and, later, of Calverley, Barham, and Locker. In its rare combination of refined raillery with subtle irony and underlying seriousness, the satire of the *Anti-Jacobin* anticipates the brilliance of *Punch* in the days when Thackeray was a contributor to its pages. The dexterous and artistic humor of Canning and his confederates did not drive out the cut-and-slash method of Gifford, but it did succeed in teaching the lesson that mockery and wit are fully as effectual as vituperation in remedying a public evil.

At the time of the subsidence of the *Anti-Jacobin* in 1798,[1] the boy Byron, just made a lord by the death of his great-uncle on May 19, 1798, was in his eleventh year. From this date on, therefore, it is necessary to take account not only of the satiric literature which may have influenced his work, but also of the events in politics and society which were occurring around him and which determined in many ways the course of his career as a satirist. From his environment and his associations came often his provocation and his material.

No single verse-satire of note was produced during the ten years just preceding *English Bards, and Scotch Reviewers*. It seemed, indeed, for a time, as if satire, fallen into feeble hands, would lose any claim to be considered as a branch of permanent literature. The increasing power of the daily newspapers and their abuse of the freedom of the press stimulated the composition of short satiric ballads and epigrams, designed to be effective for the moment, but most of them hastily conceived, carelessly executed, and speedily forgotten. The laws against libel, not consistently enforced until after the second conviction of Finnerty in 1811 and the imprisonment of the Hunt brothers in 1812, were habitually disregarded or evaded, and the utmost license of speech seems to have been tolerated, even when directed at the royal family. The ethical standard which Pope had set for satire and which had been kept in *New Morality* was now forgotten in the strife of faction and the play of personal spite. Pope had laid emphasis on style and technique, and even Mathias and Gifford had made some attempt to follow him; but the new school of satirists cared little for art. No doubt this degradation of satire may be partly attributed to the fact that the really capable writers

[1] The *Anti-Jacobin* was deserted by its original editors, largely because it was becoming too dangerous a weapon for aspiring statesmen to handle. A new journal, under the same name, was less successful.

of the time—Wordsworth, Coleridge, Scott, and Southey—
were engaged in poetry of another sort; but the result was
that satire became the property of journalists and poetasters
until Byron and Moore recovered for it some of its former
dignity.

It must not be inferred that there was a dearth of material
for destructive criticism.   Few decades of English history
have offered a more tempting opportunity to a satirist.[1]
The Napoleonic Wars, renewed in May, 1803, after the
brief Peace of Amiens (1802), were not, in spite of an occasional naval victory, resulting advantageously for England;
the disgraceful Convention of Cintra (1808) and the Wal-
cheren fiasco of 1809 had detracted from British prestige;
and the Peninsular Campaign of 1808 seemed at the time
to be a disastrous failure.   The wearisome conflict had
accentuated class differences, since, as Byron afterwards
pointed out in *The Age of Bronze*, the landed interests only
increased their wealth as the struggle continued.   Many
reforms were being agitated: Catholic Emancipation,
opposed resolutely by George III and not made a reality
until Canning became supreme; the abolition of negro
slavery, championed persistently by Wilberforce; and many
improvements in the suffrage laws, planned by Sir Francis
Burdett and a small group of liberal statesmen.   The older
leaders, Pitt and Fox, died in the same year (1806), leaving
weaker and less trusted men to fill their places; while po-

---

[1] It was the era described by Wordsworth in his sonnets *Written in
London, 1802*, and *London, 1802*, the last beginning,

> "Milton! thou should'st be living at this hour:
> England hath need of thee: she is a fen
> Of stagnant waters!   Altar, sword, and pen,
> Fireside, the heroic wealth of hall and bower,
> Have forfeited their ancient English dower
> Of inward happiness.   We are selfish men."

litical issues became confused until the establishment of the
Regency in 1811 opened the way for the long Tory administration of Lord Liverpool. Some incidents of an unusually
scandalous character aroused a general spirit of dissatisfaction. The impeachment of Melville in 1806 for alleged
peculation of funds in the naval office; the investigation in
1806 into the character of the giddy Princess Caroline,
instigated by the Prince of Wales, who had married her in
1795 and deserted her within a year; the resignation of the
Duke of York from the command of the army, following a
dramatic exposé of his relations with Mrs. Clarke and her
disposal of commissions for bribes; the duel between Castlereagh and Canning (1809)—all these were unsavory topics of
the hour. The open profligacy of the heir to the throne
drew upon him ridicule and contempt, and the frequent
recurrence of the King's malady left Englishmen in doubt
as to the duration of his reign. In such an age the ephemeral satires of the newspapers joined with the cartoons
of Gilray and Cruikshank in assailing evils and expressing
public indignation. It is, then, remarkable that no writer
of real genius should have been led to commemorate these
events in satire.

The formal satires of the decade are, for the most part,
lifeless, lacking in wit and art. The most readable of
them is, perhaps, *Epics of the Ton* (1807), by Lady Anne
Hamilton (1766–1846), divided into a Male Book and a
Female Book. It is a gallery of contemporary portraits,
in which some twenty women and seventeen men, all
prominent personages, are sketched by one familiar with
most of the current scandal in court and private life.
Although it is written in the heroic couplet, the versification
is singularly crude and careless. Structurally the work has
little discernible unity, being merely a series of satiric characterizations without connecting links, and each section
might have been printed as a separate lampoon. The intro-

ductory passage, however, contains a running survey of contemporary poetry which was not without influence on Byron. Lady Hamilton, ·clever retailer of gossip though she was, belongs to the decadent school of Pope.

In 1808 Tom Moore published anonymously *Corruption* and *Intolerance*, following them in the next year with *The Skeptic, a Philosophical Satire.* All three are satires in the manner and form of Pope; but in spite of their fervid patriotism, they are dull and heavy, and Moore, quick to recognize his failure, discreetly turned to a lighter variety of satire for which his powers were better fitted. Of other political satires of the same period, the best were excited by the notorious ministry of "All the Talents," formed by the Whigs after the death of their leader, Fox, in 1806. In *All the Talents!* (1807), Eaton Stannard Barrett (1786–1820), under the name of Polypus, undertook to undermine the ministry by assailing its members, following the methods of the *Rolliad* and using the diffuse notes which Mathias had popularized. A Whig reply appeared shortly after in *All the Blocks!* (1807) by the indefatigable W. H. Ireland (1777– 1835), which attacked the newly formed Tory ministry of Portland.

Among the nondescript formal satires of the time should be mentioned Ireland's *Stultifera Navis* (1807), a spiritless, impersonal, and general satire, which revives the form of Brandt's *Narrenschiff* (1494), introduced into English in Barclay's *Ship of Fools* (1508). A later satire of Ireland's, *Chalcographimania* (1814), in feeble octosyllabics, satirises collectors and bibliophiles. *The Children of Apollo* (1794), an anonymous satire of an earlier period, seems to have afforded Byron more than a suggestion for his *English Bards;* but he was influenced still more by the *Simpliciad* (1808), published anonymously, but actually written by Richard Mant (1776–1848), which is dedicated to the three revolutionary poets, Wordsworth, Southey, and Coleridge, and contains some unmerciful ridicule of their more absurd poems. Mant's work, the frank criticism of "a man of classical culture and of some poetic impulse,"[1] merits attention às being an almost contemporary outburst of the same general character as *English Bards*.

The ballad form reappeared in many satires arising from the troubled condition of politics[2]; but the usual tone of this work is scurrilous and commonplace, and dozens of such broadsides were composed and forgotten in a day. That any one of them had any definite influence on Byron, or on the course of satire in general, is highly improbable. What is important is that the literary atmosphere for a few years before 1809, although it produced no great satires, was surcharged with the satiric spirit, and that Byron, in his youth, must have been accustomed to the abusive personalities then common in the daily press. Conditions in his day encouraged rather than repressed destructive criticism.

This summary of English satiric verse between Dryden and Byron ends naturally with the year 1809, when the latter poet first revealed his true genius as a satirist. Something has been suggested of the wide scope and varied character of satire from the death of Pope until the end of the eighteenth century; the example of Pope has been traced through its influence on satire to the time when it degenerated in the work of Mathias and the minor rhymsters of the first decade of the new century; and the lighter classes of satire have been followed until the date when they became artistic in the poetry of the *Anti-Jacobin*. With many of these English predecessors Byron had something in common; from a few he drew inspiration and material. Although

---

[1] See the *Nation*, volume xciv., No. 2436, March 7, 1912.

[2] Examples are *Elijah's Mantle* (1807) by James Sayer (1748–1823), with its answer, the anonymous *Elijah's Mantle Parodied* (1807); the *Uti Possidetis and Status Quo* (1807), *The Devil and the Patriot* (1807), and Canning's famous ballad *The Pilot that Weathered the Storm*.

it will be possible to point out only a few cases in which he was indebted to them directly for his manner and phraseology, it was their work which determined very largely the course which he pursued as a satirist in verse.

With the appearance of *English Bards, and Scotch Reviewers*, English satire regained something of the standing which it had once had in the days of Pope and Swift. Men of the highest genius were soon to employ satire as a weapon.   Moore, the Smiths, Praed, Hood, and Hook were to carry raillery and mockery almost to the point of perfection; Shelley was to unite satire with idealism and a lofty philosophy; and Byron himself, the last master in the school of Pope, was to introduce a new variety of satire, borrowed from the Italians, and to gain for himself the distinction of being perhaps the greatest of our English verse-satirists.

CHAPTER III

Fugitive Pieces, Byron's first volume of verse, actually printed in November, 1806, was almost immediately suppressed at the instance of his elder friend and self-appointed mentor, Rev. J. T. Becher, who somewhat prudishly expostulated with him on the sensuous tone of certain passages. Of the thirty-eight separate poems which the collection contains, eight, at least, may be classed as legitimate satires. The arrangement of the different items is, however, unsystematic and inconsistent. The lines *On a Change of Masters at a Great Public School*, comprising a prejudiced and impulsive diatribe, are followed by the *Epitaph on a Beloved Friend*, a sincere and heartfelt elegy; while the conventionally sentimental *Lines to Mary, On Receiving Her Picture* are preceded and followed by satiric poems. These unexpected juxtapositions, inexplicable even on the theory of an adherence to chronology, suggest at once the curious way in which Byron's versatile and complex nature tended to show itself at various times in moods apparently antithetical, permitting them often to follow each other closely or even to exist at practically the same moment. In his early book two characteristic moods, if not more, may be recognized: the romantic, whether melancholy, sentimental, or mysterious; and the satiric, whether savage or mocking. It is, of course, only with the manifestations of the latter mood that we have here to do.

The motives which urged Byron, at this early age,

towards satire arose chiefly from personal dislike, the wish
to retaliate when some one, by word or deed, had offended
his vanity or his partialities.   His animosities, notoriously
violent, were often, though not always, hasty, irrational,
and unjustified.   His satire was occasioned by his emotions,
not by his reason, a fact which partly accounts for- his
fondness for exaggeration and his incapacity for weighing
evidence.   As to his choice of methods, it must be remembered that careful reading, of a scope and diverseness
remarkable for one of his years, had given him a comprehensive acquaintance with the English poets, and notably
with Pope, for whom his preference began early and continued long.   From Pope, and from Pope's literary de-
scendant, Gifford, Byron derived the models for much of his
preliminary work in satire.   He also knew Canning and
Mathias, Lady Hamilton, Mant, and E. S. Barrett, and, in
a different field, he was familiar with the lighter verse of
Swift, Prior, Anstey, the *Rolliad*, and the *Anti-Jacobin*.
It was natural, indeed almost inevitable, that these first
exercises in satire should reflect something of the style and
manner of poems with which Byron had an acquaintance
and of which he had made a study.

The first printed satire of his composition was the poem
entitled *On a Change of Masters at a Great Public School*,
dated from Harrow, July, 1805, when his period of residence
there had almost closed.   Dr. Drury, Headmaster of
Harrow, having resigned, Dr. Butler had been chosen to
fill the vacancy.   Against Dr. Butler, Byron had no personal grievance; but resenting an appointment which, passing over Dr. Drury's son, Mark Drury, had selected an
utter stranger, the boy launched an invective at a teacher
whom he scarcely knew, and predicted the downfall of the
school under his administration.   Characteristically enough
he was soon ready to avow his regret for his rash outburst.
Referring to Dr. Butler, he said in his Diary: "I treated him

rebelliously, and have been sorry ever since." In the details of Byron's conduct at this time are exemplified several of his traits as a satirist: impetuous judgment, energetic attack, and eventual repentance.

The use of the Latin type names, Probus and Pomposus, applied to Dr. Drury and Dr. Butler, as well as a certain technical skill in the management of the heroic couplet, indicates that Byron had perused Pope to his own advantage. Already he had caught something of the tricks of antithesis and repetition of which the elder poet had been so fond, and he had derived from him the power of condensing acrimony into a single pointed couplet. Such lines as:

> "Of narrow brain, yet of a narrower soul,
> Pomposus holds you in his harsh control;
> Pomposus, by no social virtue sway'd,
> With florid jargon, and with vain parade,"[1]

have a hint of the vigor and vehemence of Pope himself, while they display, at the same time, the unfairness and exaggerated bitterness, so rarely mitigated by good humor, which were to distinguish the longer *English Bards*.

This poem, after all, was a mere scholastic experiment to be read only by those in close touch with events at Harrow. *Fugitive Pieces* contained also Byron's earliest effort at political satire. An *Impromptu*, unsigned, and derogatory to Fox, had appeared in the *Morning Post* for September 26, 1806, only a few months after the death of the great Whig statesman, and the schoolboy, even then headed toward liberalism, came to the Minister's defence in a reply published in the *Morning Chronicle* in October of the same year. The opening couplet:

> "Oh, factious viper! whose envenomed tooth,
> Would mangle still the dead, perverting truth,"

[1] *Poetry*, i., 17.

proved that he possessed, with Gifford, the singular faculty
of working himself, with very little cause, into a furious rage.
When once he had let his wrath master him, he was uncon-
trollable, and he found satisfaction in nothing so much as in
affixing scurrilous epithets to those who had aroused him.
Until he had studied the Italian satirists, he was almost
incapable of cool dissection of an enemy's faults or short-
comings, and even then he never acquired the virtue of
self-control.

This essay at political satire was not followed by other
excursions into politics, probably because of the poet's
temporary indifference to the situation in England at the
time.   On January 15, 1809, in writing his solicitor, Hanson,
concerning his entrance into the House of Lords, he said:
"I cannot say that my opinion is strongly in favor of either
party."[1]   Not until after his return to England from his
travels in 1811 and the beginning of his friendship with
Moore, Hunt, and other active Whigs, did his interest in
politics revive and his pen become a party weapon.

The last of the three classical satires in couplets to be
found in *Fugitive Pieces* is *Thoughts Suggested by a College
Examination* (1806), composed at Cambridge.   It opens
with a burlesque sketch of Magnus, a college tutor, but
soon broadens into a general indictment of pedantry and
scholastic sycophancy.   Byron himself had desired to go to
Oxford, and he never felt himself in sympathy with either
the instructors or the educational system of his Alma Mater.
This particular poem, however, is merely an outburst of
boyish spleen, remarkable for nothing except a kind of
sauciness not unknown in the university freshman.

Fugitive Pieces had been privately printed, with the
addition of twelve poems, and with two poems omitted,
as *Poems on Various Occasions* in January, 1807, and in the
summer of the same year a new collection, consisting partly

[1] *Letters*, i., 209.

of selections from the two previous volumes and partly of hitherto unprinted work, was published under the title *Hours of Idleness.* A final edition, called *Poems Original and Translated*, appeared in 1808, comprising thirty-eight separate poems, five of them new. Among the poems in these volumes, and other verses of the same period, drawn from various sources and since gathered together in Mr. Coleridge's authoritative edition of Byron's poetry, there are several satires, many of them interesting in themselves and nearly all illuminating in their relation to the author's later production.

Childish Recollections (1806),[1] a sentimental reverie, is satiric in part, though it is devoted mostly to eulogies of Byron's companions at Harrow. In the couplet,

"Let keener bards delight in Satire's sting,
My fancy soars not on Detraction's wing,"

he disavows any satiric intent, but this does not prevent him from indulging in some additional criticism of Dr. Butler. Regret for this passage induced Byron to omit the entire poem from *Poems Original and Translated*, and in ordering the excision he wrote Ridge: "As I am now reconciled to Dr. Butler I cannot allow my satire to appear against him."

Damoetas, a short fragment of truculent characterization, may be a morbid bit of self-portraiture, but is more probably a cynical sketch of some acquaintance. The description is excessively bitter:—

"From every sense of shame and virtue wean'd,
In lies an adept, in deceit a fiend;—
Damoetas ran through all the maze of sin,
And found the goal, when others just begin."

[1] It is probable that Byron's verses are modelled somewhat on the *Epistle on His Schoolfellows at Eton* (1766) by his relative and guardian, Lord Carlisle (1748–1825).

The poems so far mentioned as composed by Byron before 1809 have been formal exercises in the manner of Pope, tentative efforts in the *genre* of which *English Bards* was to be Byron's best example.   Even in this early period, how-ever, another phase of his satiric spirit appears, which hints of the future *Don Juan;* it trifles in a lighter vein, with less of invective and more of banter, and the style is lent a humorous touch by the use of odd and uncommon rhymes. The half-genial playfulness of these poems is decidedly dif-ferent from the earnestness and intensity of *Damoetas*, and makes them akin to the familiar verse of Prior, Cowper, and Praed.   One of the cleverer specimens is the poem with the elaborate title *Lines to a Lady Who Presented to the Author a Lock of Her Hair Braided with His Own, and Ap-pointed a Night in December to Meet Him in the Garden,* in which thirteen rhymes out of twenty-two are double. These verses, printed first in *Fugitive Pieces*, are possibly the earliest in which evidence may be found of a sportive mood in Byron's work.   Their tone is both ironic and comic, and possible romance is turned into something ri-diculous by a satiric use of realism.   The poem is also one of the few examples of Byron's employment of octosyllabic couplets for satiric purposes.

To Eliza (October 9, 1806), written to Elizabeth Pigot, Byron's early correspondent and confidante, contains some cynical observations on marriage, with at least one line that might have fitted into *Don Juan :*

"Though women are angels, yet wedlock 's the devil."

It is composed in stanzas made up of four anapestic lines. *Granta, a Medley*, written October 28, 1806, in one of the bursts of rhyming not uncommon with him at that period, treats, in a jocular fashion, of college life at Cambridge.   Its chief interest lies in some of its peculiar rhymes, such as

triangle-wrangle, historic use-hypothenuse, before him-
tore 'em, crude enough in themselves, but prophetic of
better skill to come, and in the fact that it uses the common
quatrain of four-stressed lines, with alternate rhymes, a
measure seldom found in Byron's satire. *To the Sighing
Strephon*, in a six-line stanza, while occasionally serious, is
actually the reflection of a frivolous mood, and contains light
satire.   The trivial nature of these poems as contrasted with
the vehemence of some other of his early satires, indicates
that Byron's satiric spirit even at that time was fickle and
changeable, dependent often on his environment and vary-
ing constantly in response to alterations in his own temper.
It is noticeable too that he was experimenting with several
metrical forms, and trying his hand at extraordinary rhymes.

Byron's path as an aspiring author was not always a
smooth one, even before his name became generally known.
Fugitive Pieces had been harshly criticised by several of his
acquaintances, and, as we have seen, the objections of the
hypercritical Becher had led to the destruction of the
entire edition.   But the proud young lord was not always
tamely submissive to correction.   In December, 1806, he
wrote in Hudibrastic couplets the verses *To a Knot of Un-
generous Critics*, which express the same sort of injured
pride and resentment that he afterwards showed toward
Jeffrey and the Edinburgh reviewers:

> "Rail on, rail on, ye heartless crew!
> My strains were never meant for you;
> Remorseless rancour still reveal,
> And damn the verse you cannot feel."

Byron's anger in these lines was directed apparently at certain ladies of Southwell, the little town where most of his
Harrow vacations were spent; but though he mentioned one
"portly female," he had not yet reached the point where he

ventured to call his enemies by name. This reserve, however, did not prevent him from breaking out in some caustic
personal satire, in the course of which he did not spare the
characters of the ladies in question. The same provocation
led him to compose the *Soliloquy of a Bard in the Country*
(1806), in heroic couplets, in which he seems to pick three
persons—"physician, parson, dame"—as responsible for
the adverse comment on *Fugitive Pieces*. In these satires
the occasional sharpness of single phrases does not conceal
a boyish timidity, which is evidence that Byron had not
yet been stung enough to make him realize or display his full
power. Neither of the poems was published during his lifetime, and they probably served only to gratify his revenge
in private among his friends.

Possibly the last, and certainly the most cynical, of these
early satires is the well-known *Inscription on the Monument
of a Newfoundland Dog*, dated by Byron from Newstead
Abbey, October 30, 1808, though the animal did not die
until November 18th. The twenty-six lines of the poem are
now carved on a monument at Newstead, with an elaborate
prose epitaph. Their misanthropy and savagery recall
the contempt which Swift expressed for humanity in such
poems as *The Beasts' Confession* and the *Lines on the Day of
Judgment*. An appropriate text for Byron's verses might
have been taken from Swift's letter to Pope, September 29,
1725: "I heartily hate and detest that animal called man."
Doubtless Byron's mood is due in part to an affectation of
cynicism which reappeared frequently throughout his life;
his hatred of mankind, if not actually assumed, was by no
means the deep-seated emotion that agitated Swift.

A retrospective survey of the material so far considered
again fastens our attention on the singular complexity of
Byron's satiric spirit. In a body of work comparatively
meagre in content, he had used both invective and mockery,
severity and humor. He had tried various metrical forms,

some dignified and some colloquial.   There is less to be said, however, for the intrinsic merit of the satires.   No one of them is brilliant, nor does any one suggest marked intellectual power.   The invective is too often mere indiscriminate ranting; the wit is, for the most part, sophomoric; and the assumption of superiority in one so young is, at times, exceedingly offensive.   Here and there in single lines and passages, there are indications of latent genius; but many other young poets have shown as much.

These exercises, however, imitative and crude though they were, were training him in style and giving him confidence.   When his anger was fully roused by the Edinburgh Review, he found himself prepared with an instrument for his purposes.   English Bards, and Scotch Reviewers, with all its faults, is not the product of an amateur in satire, but of a writer who, after much study of the methods of Pope and Gifford, has learned how to express his wrath in virulent couplets.

CHAPTER IV

"ENGLISH BARDS, AND SCOTCH REVIEWERS"

English Bards, and Scotch Reviewers, Byron's first long poem, is, like the *Dunciad* and the *Baviad*, a satire principally on literary people. It was not, however, in its inception, planned to be either so pretentious or so comprehensive as it afterwards came to be. In a letter to Elizabeth Pigot, October 26, 1807, when Byron was still an undergraduate of Trinity College, Cambridge, he referred casually to "one poem of 380 lines, to be published (without my name) in a few weeks, with notes," and added, "The poem to be published is a satire."[1] The manuscript draft of the work as thus conceived contained 360 lines.

The actual stimulus for the enlargement of the poem came, however, from an external source. Injured vanity, the occasion of the earlier *Soliloquy of a Bard in the Country*, was also responsible for the completion of the half-formed satire of which Byron had written to Miss Pigot. On February 26, 1808, he wrote Becher: "A most violent attack is preparing for me in the next number of the *Edinburgh Review*."[2] The attack alluded to, a criticism of *Hours of Idleness*, unsigned but probably contributed by Brougham, appeared in the *Edinburgh Review* for January, 1807; but that number, in accordance with a practice not then uncommon, was delayed for over a month in going through the press, and was not actually on sale until March.

[1] *Letters*, i., 47. [2] *Letters*, i., 183.

The article itself, which has since become notorious for its bad taste, began with the scathing sentence: "The poetry of this young lord belongs to the class which neither gods nor men are said to permit." Its attitude was certainly not calculated to encourage or soothe the youthful poet, and with his usual impetuosity, he at once sought a means of redress. Adding an introduction and a conclusion to his embryonic poem, and inserting an attack on Jeffrey, whom he supposed to be his critic, he had the whole privately printed, as *British Bards*, in the autumn of 1808. This work, revised and enlarged, but with some excisions,[1] making a poem of 696 lines, was published anonymously in March, 1809, under the title *English Bards, and Scotch Reviewers*. A letter of January 25, 1809, to Dallas proves that the poet had intended to conceal his authorship by inserting a slighting reference to "minor Byron,"[2] but this ruse was not retained in the published volume.

The satire, as Byron told Medwin, made a prodigious impression. A second edition in October, 1809, was amplified by several interpolated passages so that it comprised 1050 lines. A third and a fourth edition were demanded while Byron was on his travels, and the fifth, including the 1070 lines of the poem as it is ordinarily printed to-day, was suppressed by him in 1811. In the second and succeeding editions his name was on the title-page.

His friend, Dallas, who had been favored with the perusal of the poem in manuscript, had suggested as a title, *The Parish Poor of Parnassus*, but Byron, with some wisdom, rejected this as too humorous,[3] and chose *English Bards, and Scotch Reviewers*. The present title indicates clearly the double object of the satire; for though it is, in one sense, an attempt at retaliation upon the editors of the *Edinburgh Review*, it is, in another, an eager and deliberate defence of the Popean tradition in poetry. It combines the motives

[1] *Letters*, i., 167.　　　[2] *Letters*, i., 211.　　　[3] *Letters*, i., 212.

of Churchill's *Apology* and Gifford's *Baviad* in that it aims, like the first, to castigate hostile critics, and like the second, to ridicule contemporary poets. Personal spite urged him to assail the "Scotch marauders," Jeffrey, Horner, and their coterie; but he had no individual grudge to pay in satirising the "Southern dunces," Wordsworth, Southey, Moore, and others. His attack upon them was actuated by the same sort of narrow spirit which he had condemned in his critics. The spectacle of Byron posing as an overthrower of intolerant reviewers, and in the same poem outdoing them in unjust and prejudiced criticism is not likely to leave the reader with an exalted opinion of the author's consistency.

Presumably influenced by the example of Gifford, Byron deluded himself into believing that it was his mission to protest against the excesses of romanticism in poetry, and to engage "the swarm of idiots" who were infecting literature. He was to be "self-constituted judge of poesy"; and in pursuance of his design, the satire became a gallery of many figures, some sketched graphically, others merely limned in a line or a phrase. It is to Byron's credit that his chosen victims were not, like those of Pope and Gifford, all poetasters. Doubtless there was a certain amount of chance in the causes that led him to be the opponent of men who have since been recognized as representative poets of their age; but in spite of the fact that Wordsworth and Coleridge, Southey and Moore, may not have been fully appreciated in 1809, they were, nevertheless, authors of reputation whom it was not altogether discreet to attack. As for Scott, he was the favorite writer of the period and no mean antagonist. Herford points out the daring character of the satire in saying: "It is a kind of inverted *Dunciad;* the novice falls upon the masters of his day, as the Augustan Master upon the nonentities of his."

The originality of the satire was questioned as far back

as 1822 in *Blakwood's Magazine*, which, in a *Letter to Paddy*, said: "*English Bards* is, even to the most wretched point of its rhyme, most grossly and manifestly borrowed."[1] That this is inexcusable exaggeration hardly needs asserting; yet it is not detrimental to Byron to state that he had been anticipated in many of his criticisms to such an extent that his views could have offered little of novelty to his readers, and that some of his lines are reminiscent of the work of previous English satirists. He was no direct plagiarist, but he had a tenacious memory, and he had read omnivorously in Pope, Churchill, Gifford, and the minor satirists of his own time. It is not strange that he occasionally repeats phrases which had become, by inheritance, the common property of all English satirists.

Continuing a practice which, as we have seen, was instituted by Oldham and adopted by Pope and Gifford, Byron evidently intended to follow the general plan of the first satire of Juvenal. Pope, in the *Satires and Epistles Imitated*, had printed the Latin poems of Horace in parallel columns with his own verses.[2] Gifford, in the *Baviad*, had placed sections of the text of Persius in notes at the bottom of the page, and had adhered rather closely to the structure of his Latin model. Byron, however, soon perceived the restrictions which such procedure would entail, and after indicating three examples of imitation in the first hundred lines, neglected Juvenal in order to pursue an independent course.[3] Aside from these acknowledged imitations, it is interesting to notice that one couplet from *English Bards*,

[1] *Blackwood's*, ix., 461.
[2] This practice was ridiculed by his enemy, Lady Montagu, in the lines:

> "On the one side we see how Horace thought,
> And on the other how he never wrote."

[3] The opening couplet of *English Bards* is a paraphrase of the first two lines of Juvenal, I. Other imitations occur in lines 87–88 (Juvenal, I., 17–18) and lines 93–94 (Juvenal, I., 19–21).

> "I, too, can scrawl, and once upon a time
> I poured along the town a flood of rhyme,"[1]

have some resemblance to two lines of Gifford's translation of Juvenal's first satire,

> "I, too, can write—and at a pedant's frown,
> Once poured my fustian rhetoric on the town."

These few instances excepted, there is no evidence in the poem of borrowing from the Latin satirists, nor is any one of them mentioned or quoted in *English Bards*.

It is curious that Byron, instead of striking out for himself in an original way, should have repeated complacently many of the time-honored ideas which had become almost fixed conventions in satire. It is customary, of course, for the satirist to complain of contemporary conditions and to sigh for the good old days; indeed, it would be possible to collate passages from satirists in an unbroken line from Juvenal to William Watson, each making it clear that the age in which the writer lives is decadent. As far back as 1523 we find in the verse preface to *Rede Me and be nott wrothe*, a couplet full of this lament:

> "This worlde is worsse than evyr it was,
> Never so depe in miserable decaye."

Marvell, in *An Historical Poem*, wishes for the glorious period of the Tudors; Dryden, in the *Epistle to Henry Higden, Esq.*, cries out against "our degenerate times"; and Pope, in the *Dunciad*, has a familiar reference to "these degen'rate days." The same strain is repeated in Young,[2] in Johnson,[3] in Cowper,[4] in Gifford,[5] and even in Barrett.[6]

[1] *English Bards*, 47–48.   [2] *Satires*, iii., 15–18.
[3] *London*, 35–36.   [4] *Table Talk*, 571–572.
[5] *Baviad*, 215 ff.   [6] *All the Talents*, ii., 46–47.

The tone of Byron's jeremiad differs very little from that of those which have been cited:

> "Time was, ere yet in these degenerate days
> Ignoble themes obtained mistaken praise,
> When Sense and Wit with Poesy allied,
> No fabled Graces, flourished side by side."[1]

It is not inappropriate to point out that this ideal era to which Byron refers had been termed by Pope, who lived in it, "a Saturnian Age of lead."[2] It required a maturer Byron to satirise this very satiric convention as he did in the first line of *The Age of Bronze:*

> "The 'good old times'—all times when old are good."

Another generally accepted custom for the satirist was the apologetic formality of calling upon some supposedly more powerful censor to revive and scourge folly. Thus Young had asked,

> "Why slumbers Pope, who leads the tuneful train,
> Nor hears the virtue which he loves complain."[3]

Whitehead's *State Dunces* had opened with a similar invocation to Pope. At the end of the eighteenth century it was Gifford who seemed to have sunk into a torpor. Thus we find Canning in *New Morality* attempting to rouse him:

> "Oh, where is now that promise? why so long
> Sleep the keen shafts of satire and of song?"

Hodgson, Byron's friend, in his *Gentle Alterative* had also appealed to Gifford. In the preface to the second edition of *English Bards*, Byron had, in his turn, regretted the listlessness of Gifford, and had modestly professed himself a

---

[1] *English Bards*, 103–106.   [2] *Dunciad*, i., 28.   [3] *Satires*, i., 35–36.

mere country practitioner officiating in default of the regular physician; while in the satire itself he again sounded the familiar note, repeating the interrogation of Canning:

> "'Why slumbers Gifford?' once was asked in vain;
> Why slumbers Gifford? let us ask again."[1]

The emphatic language which he used elsewhere in admitting his indebtedness and even his inferiority to Gifford is, however, proof of the sincerity of this outburst.

A third convention, established if not originated in English by Pope, is the obligation felt by the satirist to pose as a defender of public morals and to insist upon his ethical purpose. Byron, partly affected by this tradition, partly believing himself to be, like Gifford, a champion of law and order in literature, tries to persuade his public that he is instigated entirely by lofty motives in giving vent to his anger:

> "For me, who, thus unasked, have dared to tell
> My country, what her sons should know too well,
> Zeal for her honor bade me here engage
> The host of idiots that infest her age."[2]

It will not do, however, to take this assertion too seriously, especially since incitements of a far different sort seem to have occasioned several sections of the poem.

Besides conforming to the conventional practice of his predecessors in these three important respects, Byron linked himself with them by so many other ties that even in matters of minor detail *English Bards* resembles the classical satires of Pope and Gifford. As a satire it may justly be compared with the *Dunciad* and the *Baviad*, and may be judged by the standards which are applied to them.

[1] *English Bards*, 819–820.   [2] *English Bards*, 991–994.

An analysis of *English Bards* is rendered difficult by the lack of any coherent plan in the poem, and its consequent failure to follow any logical order in treating its material. The author wanders from his avowed theme to satirise the depravity of the Argyle Institution and to ridicule the antiquarian folly of Aberdeen and Elgin, slipping, moreover, easily from critics to bards and from bards to critics, as a train of observations occurs to him. The same excuse may be pleaded for him that Mathias advanced in his own behalf: that an informing personality lends a kind of unity to the poem. It may be said, too, that the classical satire, not aiming as a rule to be compact and close in structure, is very likely to become a panorama in which figures pass in long review. This impression is conveyed in *English Bards* by the use of stock phrases which serve to introduce each new character as if he were appearing in a parade of celebrities.[1]

Under the false impression that Jeffrey was responsible for the scornful review of *Hours of Idleness*, Byron singled him out for violent abuse, though he did not neglect his colleagues, "the allied usurpers on the throne of taste." For his attack on critics as a class Byron could have found much encouragement in previous English satire. Dryden had expressed a common enough feeling of authors, in the lines:

"They who write ill, and they who ne'er durst write,
Turn critics out of mere revenge and spite."[2]

Pope had condemned the "bookful blockhead, ignorantly read," who knows no method in his calling but censure.[3] Young had carried out rather tamely in his third satire his boastful intention of falling upon critics:

[1] See *English Bards*, 144–145, 165–166, 202, 235, etc.
[2] Prologue to the second part of the *Conquest of Granada*, 1–2.
[3] *Essay on Criticism*, 610–630.

"Like the bold bird upon the banks of Nile,
That picks the teeth of the vile crocodile."

Aside from these more or less incidental aspersions, at
least two entire satires had been written upon critics.
Cuthbert Shaw, enraged by what he thought an unfair
account of his *Race* (1762) in the *Critical Review*, prefixed
to the second edition of that poem an *Address to the Critics*,
in which he heaped vituperation on all the reviewers of his
time.   Only a few months before this, Churchill in his
Apology Addressed to the Critical Reviewers (1761) had con-
structed a satire very similar in motive and plan to Byron's
English Bards.   A fairly close parallel may, in fact, be
evolved between the two poems.   Both are replies to the
severe comments of critics on an earlier work[1]; both assail
Scotch editors, the victim being, in the one case, Smollett,
in the other, Jeffrey; both digress from the main theme, the
one to renew the controversy with actors begun in the
Rosciad, the other to satirise a new movement in poetry.

It is characteristic of both Churchill and Byron that,
instead of attempting to defend their verses, they devote
all their attention to reviling their reviewers.   Byron's
retaliation is less vigorous than Churchill's; indeed it may
be said that *English Bards* is weakest in the place where it
should have been most effective—in the passage directed
at Jeffrey.   Byron compares his antagonist to the hangman
Jeffries, and describes in burlesque fashion the duel between
him and Moore; but he fastens on him no epithet worth

[1] *The Apology* was written in response to a scathing article on the
Rosciad, printed in the *Critical Review* for March, 1761.   This periodical, ultra-Tory in its principles, made a point of decrying, any work
which was by a Whig author, or expressed any sympathy with liberal
ideas.   Though the editor, Tobias Smollett, was able to exculpate himself from the charge, Churchill deemed him accountable for the uncomplimentary review and, without naming him, described him in his satire
as "alien from God, and foe to all mankind."

remembering and abuses him in lines which are neither incisive nor witty.

Churchill had made an especial point of the anonymous character of the articles in the *Critical Review*, and had said of the editors:

"Wrapt in mysterious secrecy they rise,
And, as they are unknown, are safe and wise."[1]

Hodgson, in his *Gentle Alterative* (1809), had referred to a similar custom of the *Edinburgh Review*, by attacking,

"Chiefly those anonymously wise,
Who skulk in darkness from Detection's eyes."

The allusion in *English Bards* to "Northern Wolves, that still in darkness prowl"[2] may be explained by Byron's objection to this practice, though he chooses to dwell on it very little.

The Apology had accused the critics of dissimulation and had alleged that their pages were full of misstatements—

"Ne'er was lie made that was not welcome there."[3]

Byron made the same charge in advising contributors to the *Edinburgh Review* not to stick to the truth,

"Fear not to lie, 't will seem a sharper hit."[4]

It is quite apparent that the "self-elected monarchs" whom Churchill treated so cavalierly in 1761 had no more popularity among sensitive authors than did the body of critics whom Hodgson styled "self-raised arbiters of sense and wit,"[5] whom Gifford spoke of as "mope-eyed dolts placed

[1] *The Apology*, 110–111.   [2] *English Bards*, 429.
[3] *The Apology*, 44.   [4] *English Bards*, 71.   [5] *Gentle Alterative*.

by thoughtless fashion on the throne of taste"[1] and whom
Byron, in much the same phraseology, scorned as,

> "Young tyrants, by themselves misplaced,
>   Combined usurpers on the Throne of Taste."

Churchill, rash though he was, was cautious enough not
to print his opponents' names, and they are to be discovered
only through definite allusions. Byron, on the other hand,
brought his satire into the open, and ridiculed "smug
Sydney," "classic Hallam," "paltry Pillans," "blundering
Brougham," and other contributors to the *Edinburgh*, never
hesitating to give a name in full. Even Lord and Lady
Holland, later Byron's close friends, were included among
the victims, as patrons of the Whig *Review*.

These resemblances between *English Bards* and some
earlier satires of a like nature do not prove Byron a mere
imitator. Enough has been shown, perhaps, to make it
clear that his work belongs to a definite school of poetry,
and that his verses show no marked originality. At the
same time he never stoops to direct plagiarism, and whatever similarities exist with other poems are largely those
of style and spirit, not of phraseology.

But there is much more in *English Bards* than the outburst against critics; dexterously Byron proceeded himself
to don the garb of judge and to pass sentence on men older
and better known than he. He had early adopted a conservative attitude towards the versification and subject-
matter of poetry, a position which he preserved in theory
throughout his life.[2] Having learned to use glibly the
catchwords of the Augustans, he ventured to praise Crabbe,
Campbell, Rogers, and Gifford for adhering tenaciously to

---

[1] *Baviad*, 200–201.

[2] It is curious that Byron's views on poetry were not very different
from those held by Jeffrey. Both men believed in maintaining the common-sense traditions of the eighteenth century.

the principles of Sense, Wit, Taste, and Correctness established by Pope. Acting on this basis, he was justified
in condemning his own age for its disregard of what he considered to be the standard models of poetic expression.[1]
Under the tutelage of Gifford, he had acquired a distaste
for novelty which led him to look upon the romanticists
as Gifford looked upon the Della Cruscans, and which
induced him to carry his defence of custom and tradition
almost to the verge of bigotry.

Something must be allowed, too, for the operation of
contemporary ideas upon Byron. The leaders of the so-
called Romantic Movement, partly because many of them
had associated themselves with the Jacobin party in
England, partly because their poetry seemed strange, were
met from the first with opposition in many quarters.[2]
Language of a tenor hostile to their work may be met with
in Mathias, the *Anti-Jacobin*, *Epics of the Ton*, the *Simpliciad*, and Hodgson's *Gentle Alterative*. The suggestions for
many of the anti-romantic views since attributed to Byron
alone came doubtless from other satirists, whose accusations Byron fitted into telling phrases.

An excellent illustration of this is to be found in Byron's
unprovoked attack upon Scott, in which the younger poet,
seizing upon the well-known fact that Scott had received
money for his verses, terms him "hireling bard" and
"Apollo's venal son." Perhaps Byron may have shared
with Young the snobbish notions about money expressed
in the latter's couplet:

[1] "There can be no worse sign for the taste of the times than the
depreciation of Pope" (*Letters*, v, 559).

[2] W. Tooke, in his edition of Churchill's *Works* (1804), expresses one
phase of contemporary opinion in speaking of "the simplicity of a later
school of poetry, the spawn of the lakes, consisting of a mawkish combination of the nonsense verse of the nursery with the rhodomontade
of German Mysticism and Transcendentalism" (i., 189).

"His [Apollo's] sacred influence never should be sold;
'T is arrant simony to sing for gold."[1]

It is more probable, however, that he had in mind a passage
from *Epics of the Ton*, in which Scott's "well-paid lays"
had been mentioned in a contemptuous manner.[2]   Even
in his charge that the plot of the *Lay of the Last Minstrel*
was "incongruous and absurd," Byron had been anticipated
in a note to *All the Talents*.[3]   The whole tirade against
Scott in *English Bards* was particularly unfortunate because,
as was revealed later, that author had remonstrated with
Jeffrey on the "offensive criticism" of *Hours of Idleness*.

Byron's antagonism to the so-called Lake School of poets,
Wordsworth, Coleridge, and Southey, began early and continued long.   In 1809 it is improbable that he had any
acquaintance with any one of the three; yet he placed them
in a conspicuous and unenviable position in *English Bards*.
His primary motives in attacking them have already been
indicated.   Considering them as faddists who were lowering
the dignity of the author's calling and degrading poetic
style, he followed the *Simpliciad* in condemning them for
the contemptible nature of their subject-matter, for their
simple diction, for their fondness for the wild and unnatural,
and for their studied avoidance of conventionality.

Southey's first verse had appeared in 1794; while Wordsworth and. Coleridge had been really introduced to the

[1] *Epistles to Pope*, ii., 165.

[2] To this utterly unjust stricture Scott made a calm reply in his
Preface to *Marmion* (1830): "I never could conceive how an arrangement between an author and his publishers, if satisfactory to the persons
concerned, could afford matter of censure to any third party."   Certainly Byron came to be a gross offender in this respect himself, and
when, in 1819, he was haggling with Murray over the price of *Don Juan*,
these boyish censures, if they met his eye, must have roused a smile.

[3] "The plot is absurd, and the antique costume of the language is
disgusting, because it is unnatural" (*All the Talents*, page 68).

public through *Lyrical Ballads.* Opposition to them and their theories had begun to be shown almost immediately, allusions to Southey, in particular, being fairly common in satiric literature before 1809. Mathias had said ironically with reference to Southey's first poem:

> "I cannot . . .
> Quit the dull Cam, and ponder in the Park
> A six-weeks Epick, or a Joan of Arc."[1]

In the *Anti-Jacobin* Southey's poetry had been ludicrously parodied, and the members of the Lake School had been branded as revolutionists. *Epics of the Ton* had ridiculed Southey and Wordsworth,[2] and the *Simpliciad* had accused all three of "childish prattle."[3] Byron, then, was no pioneer in his satire on the romanticists, nor did he contribute anything original to the controversy. The frequency and rapidity with which Southey had published long epics had impressed others before Byron cried in *English Bards:*

> "Oh, Southey! Southey! cease thy varied song!
> A bard may chaunt too often and too long."[4]

---

[1] *Pursuits of Literature,* iv., 397–398.

[2] "Then still might Southey sing his crazy Joan,
To feign a Welshman o'er the Atlantic flown,
Or tell of Thalaba the wondrous matter,
Or with clown Wordsworth, chatter, chatter, chatter."
(*Epics of the Ton,* 31–34.)

[3] After some praise of the three poets, the dedication of the *Simpliciad* closes with the words: "I lament the degradation of your genius, and deprecate the propagation of your perverted taste."

[4] Pope, in the *Dunciad,* had bantered Sir Richard Blackmore, author of epics, in the lines:—
"All hail him victor in both gifts of song,
Who sings so loudly, and who sings so long."
(*Dunciad,* ii., 267–268.)

In this early satire Byron showed no personal animosity
towards Southey; he introduced him merely as a too prolific and too eccentric scribbler, to be jeered at rather than
hated.   The fierce feud between the two men was of a later
growth.

Picking Southey as the leader of the romanticists, Byron
treats Wordsworth as merely a "dull disciple," silly in his
choice of subjects and prosaic in his poetry, "the meanest
object of the lowly group."   Perhaps the most striking defect in the satire levelled at this poet is the lack of any
recognition of his ability, an omission all the more noticeable because Byron, in the last two cantos of *Childe Harold*,
was influenced so strongly by Wordsworth's conception of
the relation between man and nature.   Coleridge receives
even less consideration.   He is "the gentle Coleridge—to
turgid ode and tumid stanza dear," and is ridiculed mainly
because of his *Lines to a Young Ass*, a poem which had
previously excited the mirth of the *Simpliciad*.[1]   The slashing manner in which the boy satirist disposes of his great
contemporaries is almost unparalleled.[2]

Byron's satire on the Rev. Samuel Bowles (1762–1850)
illustrates one phase of his veneration for Pope, and connects him with another Pope enthusiast, Gifford.   In the
Baviad Gifford had gone out of his way to confront and
refute Weston, who, in an article in the *Gentleman's Magazine*, had adduced evidence to prove that Pope's moral
character was not above reproach.   Gifford, unable to

The possibility that Byron may have had this passage in mind is
increased by his note to his lines in *English Bards*: "Must he [Southey]
be content to rival Sir Richard Blackmore in the quantity as well as the
quality of his verse?"

[1] *Simpliciad*, 212–213.

[2] It must be remembered, however, that practically every charge that
Byron brings against the "Lakists" has a counterpart in Mant's
Simpliciad, printed only a year before Byron's poem.

dispute the validity of the facts, had contented himself with describing the critic as "canker'd Weston," and terming him in a note "this nightman of literature."[1] Bowles, whose early sonnets (1789) had attracted the admiration of Coleridge, published in 1807 an edition of Pope's *Works* in ten volumes, in which he followed Weston in not sparing the infirmities and mendacities of the great Augustan. The effect of this work on Byron was like that of Weston's on Gifford, and the result was that Bowles was pilloried in *English Bards* as "the wretch who did for hate what Mallet did for hire." Nor did the quarrel end here. It grew eventually into a heated controversy between Bowles and Byron, carried on while the latter was in Italy, in the course of which Byron was provoked into calling Pope "the great moral poet of all times, of all climes, of all feelings, and of all stages of existence."[2] So strongly did he feel on the matter that he wrote, even as late as 1821, concerning *English Bards:* "The part which I regret the least is that which regards Mr. Bowles, with reference to Pope."[3] Byron's exaltation of Pope was made a positive issue in the unreserved commendation which he gave to Campbell, Rogers, and Crabbe, all three of whom were, in most respects, firm in their allegiance to that master's principles of poetry.

An odd freak of fancy led Byron to pose in *English Bards* as a watchful guardian of morality in literature, though even at that date he was the author of verses which are not altogether blameless. That he should upbraid Monk Lewis, Moore, and Strangford as "melodious advocates of lust" may well seem extraordinary to the reader who recalls the poem which Byron sent to Pigot, August 10, 1806, asking that it be printed separately as "improper for the perusal of ladies."[4] The truth is that Byron was again treading in

[1] *Baviad*, 248–261.   [2] *Letters*, v, 590.
[3] *Letters*, v., 539.   [4] *Letters*, i., 104.

the steps of others. The virtuous but somewhat prurient Mathias, excited by Lewis's novel *Ambrosio, or the Monk* (1795), which has given the writer notoriety and a nickname, had assailed the author in *Pursuits of Literature*,[1] and the supposed voluptuousness of the story had not escaped the notice of the *Anti-Jacobin* and *Epics of the Ton*. Byron had thus more than one precedent for his ironic reference to Lewis's "chaste descriptions." Moore's *Epistles, Odes, and other Poems* (1806) had been censured by the *Edinburgh Review* in an article which described Moore as "the most licentious of modern versifiers." *All the Talents* had questioned Moore's morality, and *Epics of the Ton* had mentioned a writer who,

"Like Tommy Moore has scratch'd the itching throng,
And tickled matrons with a spicy song."

Byron had been a delighted reader of the Irish poet and had been influenced by him in the more sentimental verses of *Hours of Idleness;* nevertheless he repeated the imputations of the other satirists in referring to him as

"Little! young Catullus of his day,
As sweet, but as immoral, as his lay."

To Viscount Strangford (1780–1855), of whose translation of Camoëns he had formerly been very fond, Byron offered advice:

"Be warm, but pure; be amorous, but be chaste."

In the same vein as this grave admonition are the remarks which the poet makes upon the Argyle Institution, founded

---

[1] Mathias had asserted that Moore "had neither scrupled nor blushed to depict, and to publish to the world, the arts of systematic seduction, and to thrust upon the nation the most open and unqualified blasphemy against the very code and volume of our religion" (*Pursuits of Literature,* Preface to Dialogue IV.).

by Colonel Greville as a resort for gambling and dancing. Digressing for a while without any logical reason, Byron proceeds to condemn social follies, especially those fostered by "blest retreats of infamy and ease." The passage includes some lines on round dancing, which anticipate Bryon's attack on that amusement in his later satire, *The Waltz*.

Gifford's *Mæviad*, after making some final thrusts at the Della Cruscans, had shifted its attack to contemporary actors and dramatists. That satire upon them was justified may be gathered from Gifford's remark in his Preface: "I know not if the stage has been so low since the days of Gammer Gurton as at this hour."[1] During the fifteen years following the date of this statement it cannot be averred that circumstances made it any the less applicable to the theatrical situation in England, and Byron, in 1809, in ridiculing the "motley sight" which met his eyes on the stage of his time, had perhaps even more justification than Gifford had had in 1794.[2]

Of the dramatists whom Gifford had mentioned with disfavor, only two, Frederick Reynolds (1784–1841) and Miles Andrews (died 1814), were selected for notice by Byron. What the *Mæviad* had called "Reynolds' flippant trash" was still enjoying some vogue, and *English Bards* took occasion to speak of the author as "venting his 'dammes!' 'poohs!' and 'zounds!'"[3] Miles Andrews, whose "Wonderworking poetry" had been laughed at in the *Baviad*, was barely mentioned by Byron as a writer who "may live in

[1] Preface to *Mæviad*, page 59, Note.

[2] See the account of this period in Thorndike's *Tragedy*, chapter x.

[3] Byron may have taken a suggestion from some lines of *Children of Apollo:*

> "But in his diction Reynolds grossly errs;
> For whether the love hero smiles or mourns,
> 'T is oh! and ah! and oh! by turns."

prologues, though his dramas die." In general the satire on the stage in *English Bards* consists of uninteresting remarks on some mediocre dramatists, among them Theodore Hook (1788-1841), Andrew Cherry (1762-1812), James Kenney (1780-1849), Thomas Sheridan (1775-1817), Lumley Skeffington (1762-1850), and T. J. Dibdin (1771-1841). It is a fair contention that this digression is the dreariest portion of the poem. The interpolated lines on the Italian Opera, sent to Dallas, February 22, 1809, after an evening spent at a performance, attack that amusement on the ground of its indecency. They are akin in spirit to similar passages in Young,[1] Pope,[2] Churchill,[3] and Bramston.[4]

The satire on less-known poets is indiscriminate and not always discerning. Erasmus Darwin (1731-1802), who, in his *Botanic Garden* (1789-92), was a decadent imitator of Pope, is contemptuously dismissed as "a mighty master of unmeaning rhyme." Another once popular bard, William Hayley (1745-1820), still remembered as the friend and biographer of Cowper, is branded with a stinging couplet:

> "His style in youth or age is still the same,
> Forever feeble and forever tame."

The Della Cruscans are passed over as already crushed by Gifford, and "sepulchral Grahame," "hoarse Fitzgerald," the Cottles from Bristol, Maurice, and the cobbler poets, Blackett and Bloomfield, get only a fleeting sneer. H. J. Pye, the laureate, once a butt of Mathias, is mentioned only once.

Two characterizations, however, are distinguished above the others by their singular virulence. The first was a vicious onslaught on Lord Carlisle, the friend of Fox, Byron's relative and guardian, who had been included

---

[1] *Satires*, iii., 197.
[2] *Dunciad*, iv., 45-70.
[3] *Rosciad*, 723-728.
[4] *The Man of Taste*.

among the sentimental rhymsters in Tickell's *Wreath of Fashion*. To him his ward had dedicated *Poems Original and Translated;* but the peer's carelessness about introducing Byron into the House of Lords had irritated the young poet, and he changed what had previously been a flattering notice in *English Bards* into a ferocious assault:

"The puny schoolboy and his early lay
Men pardon, if his follies pass away;
But who forgives the Senior's ceaseless verse,
Whose hairs grow hoary as his rhymes grow worse."

The sharpest satire in the poem was inserted merely to satisfy a personal grudge. Hewson Clarke (1787–1832), editor of *The Satirist*, a monthly magazine, had made sport of *Hours of Idleness* in an issue for October, 1807, and had harshly reviewed *Poems Original and Translated* in August, 1808. Byron replied in a passage full of violent invective, describing Clarke as

"A would-be satirist, a hired Buffoon,
A monthly scribbler of some low Lampoon."[1]

These lines Byron never repudiated; he appended to them in 1816 the note: "Right enough: this was well deserved and well laid on."[2]

[1] One line of Byron's attack,

"Himself a living libel on mankind,"

recalls Murphy's address to Churchill,

"Thy look 's a libel on the human race."

[2] In the *Scourge*, a new venture of Clarke's begun in 1810, that editor published another scurrilous attack on Byron, involving also the poet's mother. An action for libel which Byron intended to bring was for some reason abandoned, though not without some caustic words from him about "the cowardly calumniator of an absent man and a defenceless woman" (*Letters*, i., 324).

English Bards closes with a defiance and a challenge.
The poet, then only twenty-one, repeating that his only
motive has been "to sternly speak the truth," dares his
opponents to meet him in the open and declares his willing-
ness to engage them.   There is something amusing in the
pompous way in which Byron, throwing down the gauntlet,
boasts of his own indifference and callousness to criticism.
He had, however, achieved at least one of his two objects:
he had answered hostile reviewers in a manner which made
it plain that he would not submit unresistingly to supercilious comment on his work.   Assuredly he had turned the
weapons of his critics against themselves.

Nothing was more natural than that Byron, his wrath
for the most part evaporated, should regret his bitterness
in cases where his hasty judgment had carried him too far.
On his way home from Greece he wrote Dallas: "At this
period when I can think and act coolly, I regret that I have
written it."[1]   The story of the events leading to the sup-
pression of the fifth and last edition may be given in the
words of Byron to Leigh Hunt, October 22, 1815: "I was
correcting the fifth edition of E. B. for the press, when
Rogers represented to me that he knew Lord and Lady
Holland would not be sorry if I suppressed any further
publication of that poem; and I immediately acquiesced,
and with great pleasure, for I had attacked them upon a
fancied and false provocation, with many others; and neither was, nor am, sorry to have done what I could to stifle
that furious rhapsody."[2]   The result was that the whole
impression of this edition was burned, only a few copies
being rescued, and when, in 1816, Byron left England
forever, he signed a Power of Attorney forbidding republi-
cation in any form.[3]   His mature opinion of the work is

---

[1] *Letters*, i., 314.   See also Letters, ii., 312; iii., 192.
[2] *Letters*, ii., 326.   [3] *Letters*, v., 539.

expressed in a comment written at Diodati in 1816: "The greater part of this Satire I most sincerely wish had never been written—not only on account of the injustice of some of the critical and some of the personal part of it—but the tone and temper are such as I cannot approve."

It now remains to compare *English Bards* with other examples of English classical satire, if one may apply that title to poems which use the heroic couplet and follow the methods employed by Pope. Byron's versification in his early satires shows the effect of a careful study of Pope. It is singularly free from double rhymes, there being but five instances of them in *English Bards*.[1] Byron was somewhat more sparing than Pope in his use of the run-on line. Adopting as a basis of judgment the conclusion of Mr. Gosse that "with occasional exceptions, the presence or want of a mark of punctuation may be made the determining element," we find that, of the 1070 lines in *English Bards*, approximately 101 are of the run-on variety, that is, about ten out of every hundred. In Mr. Gosse's collation of typical passages from other poets, he estimates that Dryden has 11, Pope 4, and Keats 40 run-on lines out of every hundred. In the whole length of Byron's poem there is but one run-on couplet; in a hundred consecutive lines selected by Mr. Gosse, Dryden has one such example and Pope none. Twice Byron employs the triplet,[2] and he has two alexandrines.[3] The medial cæsura after the 4th, 5th, or 6th foot of the line occurs with great regularity as it does in Pope's work. There are a few minor peculiarities in rhyming,[4] but in general the rhymes are pure. In summarizing, it is safe to say that Byron adhered closely to the metrical principles established by Pope. Not until Hunt, Keats, and Shelley introduced the looser and less monotonous

[1] *English Bards*, 209–210; 231–232; 239–240; 253–254; 909–910.
[2] *Ibid.*, 415–417; 684–686. [3] *Ibid.*, 417, 1022.
[4] *Ibid.*, 608–609; 624–625; 656–657.

system of versification used in *Rimini, Endymion,* and *Epipsychidion,* was the heroic couplet freed from the shackles with which Pope had bound it.

Byron's candid acknowledgment that, in *English Bards,* he was venturing "o'er the path which Pope and Gifford trod before" suggests at once a comparison of his work with that of the two earlier authors. Although the *Dunciad* and *English Bards* are alike in that they are in the same metre and actuated by much the same motive, there are many differences in execution between the poems. The *Dunciad* is, as the Preface of "Martinus Scriblerus" states, a true mock-heroic, with a fable "one and entire" dealing with the Empire and the Goddess of Dulness, with machinery setting forth a "continued chain of allegories," and with a succession of incidents and episodes imitated from epic writers. *English Bards,* beginning as a paraphrase of Juvenal, has no real action and is composed of a series of descriptions and characterizations, joined by some necessary connective material. Pope's method of satire is frequently indirect: he involves his victims in the plot, making them ridiculous through the situations in which he places them. Instead of inveighing against Blackmore, Pope pictures him as victor in a braying contest. Byron, on the other hand, uses this method only once in *English Bards*— in burlesquing the duel between Jeffrey and Moore. Instinctively he prefers taking up his adversaries one by one and covering each with abuse. The *Dunciad,* with rare exceptions, assails only personal enemies of the satirist, and these, for the most part, men already despised and defenceless; Byron attacks many prominent writers of whom he knows nothing except their work, and against whom he has no grievance of a private nature. Thus in plan and operation the two satires present some striking divergences.

So far as matters of detail are concerned, *English Bards* is not always in the manner of the *Dunciad* and the other satires of Pope. It has been observed of Dryden, and occasionally of Pope, that at its best their satire, however much it may be aimed at particular persons, tends to become universal in its application, just as had been the case with the finest work of the Latin satirists. Horace's Bore, for instance, was doubtless once a definite Roman citizen; Dryden's Buckingham has a place in history: but the satire on them is pointed and effective when applied to their counterparts in the twentieth century. The same is true of Pope's Atticus, who is described in language which is both specific and general, fitted both to Addison and to a definite type of humanity. The faculty of thus creating types was not part of Byron's art. For one thing, he seldom, except in some of his earliest satires, employs type names, and he carefully prints in full, without asterisks or blank spaces, the names of those whom he attacks. His accusations are too precise to admit of transference to others, and his epithets, even when they are unsatisfactory, cannot be dissevered from the one to whom they apply. The satire on Wordsworth, illustrated as it is by quotations and by references to that author's poetry, is appropriate to him alone, and would have soon been forgotten had it not been for the eminence of the victim. It is otherwise with Pope's description of Sporus, which is often applied to others, even when it is forgotten that the original Sporus was Lord Hervey.

In many respects Byron had more in common with Gifford than with Pope. It is Gifford to whom, in *English Bards*, he refers so often as a master; it is he whom he mentions in 1811 as his "Magnus Apollo"[1]; and it was of the *Baviad* and the *Mæviad* that he was thinking when he conceived his plan of hunting down the "clamorous brood of Folly."

[1] *Letters*, ii., 27.

Pope, preserving in his satire a calm deliberation which enabled him both to conceal and to concentrate his inward wrath, was capable, even when most in a rage, of a sustained analysis of those whom he hated, and seldom let his temper sweep him off his feet. Gifford and Byron prefer a more slashing and a less reserved method. Dallas once said of Byron: "His feelings rather than his judgment guided his pen."[1] The same idea was also expressed by the poet himself:—"Almost all I have written has been mere passion."[2] These two statements, confirming each other, explain the lack of poise and the want of a sense of proportion which are apparent in *English Bards*, as they were apparent in the *Baviad*. Unlike Dryden, neither Gifford nor Pope allows his victims any merit; each paints entirely in sombre colors, without ever perfecting a finished sketch or alleviating the black picture with the admission of a single virtue. Their conclusions, naturally, are unpleasantly dogmatic, founded as they are on prejudice and seldom subjected to reason. Most satire is, of course, biassed and unjust, but the careful craftsman takes good care that his charges shall have a semblance of plausibility and shall not defeat their purpose by arousing in reaction a sympathy for the defendant.[3] Satire written in a rage is likely to be mere invective, and invective, even when embodied in artistic form, is usually less effective than deliberate irony. Byron in his later satire learned better than to portray an enemy as all fool or all knave.

Gifford was, as he sedulously protested, fighting for a principle, aiming at the extermination of certain forms of affectation and false taste in poetry. There is no ground for suspecting his sincerity, any more than there is for questioning Byron's motive in his effort to defend the classical standards against the encroachments of roman-

[1] *Recollections of Lord Byron*, page 31.   [2] *Letters*, iv., 488.
[3] See *Pope and the Art of Satire*, by G. K. Chesterton.

ticism. It so happened that Gifford was performing a genuine service to letters, while Byron engaged himself in a struggle at once unnecessary and hopeless. In their zeal and enthusiasm, however, both satirists lost a feeling for values. Gifford delivered sledge-hammer blows at butterflies; Byron classed together, without discernment, the work of mediocrity and genius, and heaped abuse indiscriminately upon poetaster and poet.

Gifford's method, like Byron's, was descriptive and direct, and his satires have little action. The *Baviad*, with its dialogue framework, is not unlike some of Pope's *Epistles*, while the *Mæviad* is more akin to *English Bards*. Byron, following Mathias and Gifford, employed prose notes to reinforce his verse, but he never, like Gifford, padded them with quotations from the men whom he was attacking. In both the *Mæviad* and *English Bards* names are printed in full. Gifford used no type names, nor did he succeed in creating a type. In style and diction Byron is Gifford's superior. The latter was often vulgar and inelegant, and his ear for rhythm and melody was poor. Byron's instinctive good taste kept him from blotting his pages with the language of the streets. His study of Pope, moreover, had enabled him to acquire something of the smoothness as well as of the vigor of that master.

It may be said in general of *English Bards* that it owes most in versification to Pope, and most in manner and structure to Gifford. There are, however, other satirists to whom Byron may have been slightly indebted. At the time when he was preparing *British Bards*, Francis Hodgson (1781–1852), his close friend, irritated by some severe criticism in the *Edinburgh Review* on his translation of Juvenal (1807), was planning his *Gentle Alterative prepared for the Reviewers*, which appeared in *Lady Jane Grey; and other Poems* (1809). The fact that the provocation was the same as for *English Bards* and that the two authors were acquain-

tances offers a curious case of parallelism in literature. It
is certain, however, that Byron's satire, which is much
longer than the *Gentle Alterative*, is indebted to it only in
minor respects, if at all.   Both satires mention the ludicrous
mistake of an *Edinburgh Review* article in attributing to
Payne Knight some Greek passages really quoted from
Pindar; but this error had been discussed in a long note to
All the Talents, and was a favorite literary joke of the period.
Both poets, too, call upon the master, Gifford, to do his
part in castigating the age. Beyond these superficial
similarities, it may safely be asserted that Byron borrowed
nothing from Hodgson.

It is curious that the striking simile of the eagle shot by
an arrow winged with a feather from his own plume used by
Moore in *Corruption*[1] should have been employed by Byron[2]
in speaking of the tragic death of Henry Kirke White
(1785–1805), the religious poet and protégé of Southey.
The simile, which has been traced to *Fragment 123* of
Æschylus, occurs also in Waller's *To a Lady Singing a Song
of His Own Composing*. It is somewhat remarkable that
two poets in two successive years should have happened
upon the same figure, each working it out so elaborately.
Aside from this one parallelism, Moore's early satires,
almost entirely political, would seem to have had no definite
influence upon *English Bards*.

It has been shown, then, that Byron's ideas in his satire
were not always entirely his own, and that he reflected,
in many cases, the views and sometimes the phraseology
of other satirists, notably Pope, Churchill, and Gifford.
English Bards belongs to the school of English classical
satire, and, as such, has the peculiarities and the established
features common to the different types of that *genre*. In
the preface to the second edition of his poem, Byron said:
"I can safely say that I have attacked none personally, who

---

[1] *Corruption*, 93–98.   [2] *English Bards*, 841–848.

did not commence on the offensive."[1] To accept this
literally would be to misinterpret Byron's whole theory of
satire. Whether he admitted it or not he was a great personal satirist—in *English Bards*, primarily a personal
satirist. Looking back at the time when his wrath was
fiercest, he said: "Like Ishmael, my hand was against all
men, and all men's against me."[2] Even when satirising
a principle or a movement, he was invariably led to attack
the individuals who represented it. Swift's satiric code:

> "Malice never was his aim;
> He lash'd the vice, but spar'd the name;
> No individual could resent,
> Where thousands equally were meant,"

was exactly contrary to Byron's practice. He sought
always to contend with persons, to decide questions, not by
argument, but by a hand-to-hand grapple.

The peculiar features of *English Bards* are to be explained
by the author's character. He did not let his reason rule.
From notes and letters we learn that he was often in doubt
whether to praise or censure certain minor figures: it was
on the spur of the moment that he changed "coxcomb Gell"
to "classic Gell." He was courageous and aggressive, but
he was also unfair and illogical. There is little real humor
in *English Bards*, so little that one is inclined to wonder
where Jeaffreson discovered the "irresistibly comic verse"
of which he speaks. When the satirist tries to be playful,
the result is usually brutality. He has not yet acquired
the conversational railling mood which he utilized so
admirably in *Beppo*.

In spite of its crudities, its lack of restraint, and its
manifest prejudices, *English Bards* shows many signs of
power. In the light of the greater satire of *Don Juan*, it

---

[1] *Poetry*, i., 291.   [2] *Letters*, ii., 330.

seems immature and inartistic, but it surpasses any work of a similar kind since the death of Pope. It is Byron's masterpiece in classical satire. To excel it he had to turn for inspiration to another quarter, and to change both his method and his style.

CHAPTER V

ON July 2, 1809, Byron, accompanied by his friend, John Cam Hobhouse, sailed from Falmouth for Lisbon on a trip that was to take him to Spain, Malta, Greece, and Turkey. When he returned to England in July, 1811, after two years of travel and adventure, he brought with him "4000 lines of one kind or another," including the first two cantos of *Childe Harold* and two satires, *Hints from Horace* and *The Curse of Minerva*. *Hints from Horace*, written in March, 1811, during the poet's second visit to Athens, is dated March 14, 1811, on the last page of the most authentic manuscript. It was composed at the Capuchin Convent in Athens, where he had met accidentally with a copy of Horace's epistle *Ad Pisones, De Arte Poetica*, commonly known as the *Ars Poetica*.

The history of the fortunes of this work is perhaps worth relating. Byron, on his arrival, handed it over at once to Dallas, without giving him a hint of *Childe Harold;* indeed, only the latter's obvious disappointment induced the poet to show him the *Pilgrimage*, which then seemed of little importance to its author. On September 4, 1811, Byron requested Dallas to aid him in correcting the proofs of *Hints from Horace*, and "in adapting the parallel passages of the imitation in such places to the original as may enable the reader not to lose sight of the allusion."[1] There is, however, no reason for thinking that Dallas actually undertook the

[1] *Letters*, ii., 24.

77

task, for on October 13th Byron complained to Hodgson that the labor of editing was still hanging fire, and begged the latter to assist him.   Shortly after, owing partly to the adverse criticism of Dallas, and partly to Murray's wish not to endanger the success of *Childe Harold*, the idea of immediate publication was put aside for some years.   In 1820, Byron, then resident in Italy, was reminded of his unprinted satire, and wrote Murray to inform him that the manuscript had been left, among various papers, with Hobhouse's father in England.[1]   At intervals he expressed anxiety about the proofs, which Murray, exercising his discretion, delayed sending.   From this revived project Byron was, for a time, dissuaded by the wise counsel of Hobhouse, who suggested that the poem would require much revision. Nevertheless on January 11, 1821, he informed Murray that he saw little to alter,[2] and accused him of having neglected to comply with his orders.   A postscript to a letter of February 16, 1821, indicates that he was contemplating printing the *Hints* with its Latin original.[3]   After March 4, 1822, there is no further allusion to the satire in his correspondence, and the question of printing it seems to have been forgotten.   Although a few selections, amounting to 156 lines, were inserted in Dallas's *Recollections* (1824), the poem did not appear complete until the *Works* were published by Murray in 1831.

Hints from Horace, through a curious perversity of judgment, was always a great favorite with Byron, and was estimated by him as one of his finest performances.   His mature opinion of it and a possible cause for his preference are given in a letter to Murray, March 1, 1821: "Pray request Mr. Hobhouse to adjust the Latin to the English: the imitation is so close that I am unwilling to deprive it of its principal merit—its closeness.   I look upon it and my Pulci

---

[1] *Letters*, iv., 425.   [2] *Letters*, v., 221.   [3] *Letters*, v., 245.

as by far the best things of my doing."[1]   On September 23,
1820, when he had published portions of his masterpiece, *Don
Juan*, he said, referring to the period of *Hints from Horace:*
"I wrote better then than now."[2]   No intelligent reader
will be likely to agree with Byron's preposterous verdict on
his own work, for *Hints from Horace*, although designed as
a sequel to *English Bards*, is so much less vigorous and brilliant that it suffers decidedly by a comparison with the
earlier satire.   The poet, far from the scenes and associations where his rage had been aroused, has lost the angry
inspiration which raised *English Bards* above mere ranting,
and the white heat of his passion has cooled with the flight
of time.   The praise which Byron bestowed upon his poem
is additional testimony to the often repeated assertion that
authors are incompetent critics of their own productions.

Byron's boastful claim for the accuracy of *Hints from
Horace* as a version of the *Ars Poetica* may possibly lead
to some misconceptions.   Professor A. S. Cook, in his *Art
of Poetry*, has pointed out some particular passages in which
the English poet imitated his model, and has proved that he
followed Horace, in places, with reasonable closeness.   But
Hints from Horace is far from being, like Byron's version
of the first canto of Pulci's *Morgante Maggiore*, a mere translation.   It must be remembered that Byron, in his secondary title, defined the *Hints* in three different ways in as
many manuscripts, as "an Allusion," as an "Imitation,"
and as a "Partial Imitation."   The fact seems to be that
the work conforms, in general, to the structure and argument of the *Ars Poetica*, in many cases translating literally
the phrasing of the original, but altering and reorganizing
the satire to fit current conditions.

The idea of thus preserving the continuity of Horace's
poem, while revising and readapting its text, was probably
first conceived by Oldham in his English version of the *Ars*

<hr>

[1] *Letters*, v., 255.   [2] *Letters*, v., 77.

Poetica. In his preface Oldham stated his design as follows: "I resolved to alter the scene from Rome to London, and to make Use of English Names of Men, Places, and Customs, where the Parallel would decently permit, which I conceived would give a kind of New Air to the Poem, and render it more agreeable to the Relish of the Present Age." Accordingly, while keeping roughly to the text of Horace, he introduced plentiful references to English poets. Byron also gives his satire a modern setting, but in so doing, takes more liberties than Oldham. He substitutes Milton for Homer as the classic example of the epic poet; he makes Shakspere instead of Æschylus the standard writer of drama. He inserts many passages, such as the remarks on the Italian Opera, on Methodism, and on the versification of *Hudibras*, which have no counterparts in the *Ars Poetica.* Oldham had refrained from satirising his contemporaries; Byron improves every opportunity for assailing his old antagonists. Allusions to "Granta" and her Gothic Halls, to "Cam's stream," to Grub-street, and to Parliament make *Hints from Horace* a thoroughly modern poem. We may apply to it Warburton's comment on Pope's *Imitations:* "Whoever expects a paraphrase of Horace, or a faithful copy of his genius, or manner of writing . . . will be much disappointed." Byron restates, without much alteration, the critical dicta which Horace had established as applicable to poetry in all times and countries; he takes the plan of the *Ars Poetica* as a rough guide for his English adaptation; but he introduces so many digressions and changes so many names that his satire is firmly stamped with his own individuality.

There is no ground for supposing that any one of the scores of translations and imitations of the *Ars Poetica* had ever met Byron's eye[1]; the nearest prototypes in English

[1] There have been many actual translations of the *Ars Poetica* into English. T. Drant published, in 1567, the first complete version.

poetry of *Hints from Horace* are probably Pope's *Essay on Criticism* and *Epistle to Augustus*. Certain superficial resemblances have led critics to the inference that Pope's *Essay* is accountable for much of Byron's *Hints*. It is remarkable that the two authors, born just a century apart, should have attempted satires so similar in tone at ages approximately the same. Pope's *Essay on Criticism*, composed probably in 1709, was printed in 1711, a hundred years before Byron wrote *Hints from Horace*. In this work Pope tried to do for criticism what Horace had done for poetry: that is, to codify and express in compact form some generally accepted principles of the art. Pope, however, saw fit to introduce incidentally some conventional precepts concerning the subject-matter of literary criticism, borrowing them from Horace, and Horace's French imitator, Boileau. Thus in Pope's *Essay* are to be found many of the maxims which Byron transferred into *Hints from Horace* from the Latin source. The correspondence between such passages in the *Essay* and their counterparts in *Hints from Horace* has led Weiser to conclude, from a study of parallel ideas, that Byron's poem is based, to a large extent, on Pope's work.[1] His thesis, however, has been all but conclusively refuted by Levy, who shows that in the nine instances of parallelism adduced by Weiser as evidence, the

---

Queen Elizabeth left a fragmentary version of 194 lines in her *Englishings* (1598). Ben Jonson's excellent *Horace, of the Art of Poetry* was printed after his death. Of other translations, from that of Roscommon (1680) in blank verse, to that of Howes (1809) in heroic couplets, it is unnecessary to speak, except to say that they mount into the hundreds. In such works as *The Art of Preaching* by Christopher Pitt (1699–1748) and *The Art of Politicks* (1731) by James Bramston (1694–1744) the title and method of Horace had been transferred to other fields. *Harlequin-Horace; or the Art of Modern Poetry* by James Miller (1706–1744) is an ironical parody of the *Ars Poetica*.

[1] See his treatise, *Ueber das Verhaltnis von Byrons Hints from Horace zu Horaz und Pope*.

lines quoted from *Hints from Horace* are really much closer
to lines from the *Ars Poetica* than they are to the citations
from the *Essay on Criticism*.[1]   Undoubtedly there are couplets in the *Hints* that recall the *Essay;* but in view of Byron's
specific statement of his obligation to Horace, it would be
rash to assume that Pope's influence was more than a
general one, the natural result of Byron's careful study of
his style and manner.   Pope's *Epistle to Augustus*, a paraphrase of Horace's Book II, Epistle I, is, in several respects,
not unlike *Hints from Horace*.   It pursues the same method
in substituting English names for Greek and Roman ones,
and in replacing classical references by allusions to contemporary life.   Moreover the *Epistle*, with its judgment on
English writers, its criticism of the drama, and its estimate
of the age, is structurally more akin to *Hints from Horace*
than is ordinarily supposed.

It would be superfluous to attempt to add anything to
Professor Cook's work in outlining the instances in which
Byron merely translated Horace.   A single illustration
will suffice to show how the same Latin lines were treated by
Pope, and, later, by Byron.   Horace's counsel:—

> "Vos exemplaria Græca
> Nocturna versate manu, versate diurna"[2]

is paraphrased roughly in the *Essay on Criticism* as,

> "Be Homer's works your study and delight,
> Read them by day and meditate by night."[3]

In this case Byron's version,

> "Ye who seek finished models, never cease
> By day and night to read the works of Greece,"[4]

is slightly more literal.

[1] See his article in *Anglia*, ii., 256.   [2] *Ars Poetica*, 269–270.
[3] *Essay on Criticism*, 124–125.   [4] *Hints from Horace*, 423–424.

Horace's treatise, technically an epistle, suffers from a want of coherence. In plan it is merely a group of maxims, with illustrations and amplifications. *Hints from Horace* is even more muddled and formless. It is like a collection of detached thoughts in verse, with each single observation jotted down almost at haphazard without regard to what comes before or after. It is no exaggeration to say that whole sections of the satire might be lifted bodily from one page to another without perceptibly affecting the continuity of thought. This defect, obscured in Horace and Pope by the epigrammatic brilliancy of separate phrases and the lift of "winged words," has, in Byron's poem, few counterbalancing virtues. *Hints from Horace* lacks the finished perfection of style which distinguishes the *Ars Poetica* and the *Epistle to Augustus*. Its versification is, except in isolated lines, feeble and careless, far inferior to that of *English Bards*, and even sinking at times, as in the passage on *Hudibras*,[1] into bare prosing. One finds in the poem confirmation of Byron's confession to Lord Holland in 1812: —"Latterly, I can weave a nine-line stanza faster than a couplet, for which measure I have not the cunning."[2] If the dates furnished by the poet are correct, 722 lines, at least, of the satire must have been composed in two weeks, a speed which may explain some of the defects in execution. Certainly, even with due allowance for Byron's strange fondness, it must be considered one of his poorest works in structure, diction, and versification.

Nor can it, viewed merely as a medium for satire, claim a high rank. It is too obviously didactic in its purpose and too general in its attacks. It does not even possess the special interest which attaches to *English Bards* because of the references to contemporary and famous writers in the latter work. Only a few lines are devoted to personal satire, and these seldom do more than repeat or amplify the

[1] *Hints from Horace*, 399–412.   [2] *Letters*, ii., 150.

criticism embodied in the earlier poem.   The result is that
Hints from Horace, taken as a satire only, is open to a charge
of futility, in that its motive is not definite and its satire is
too scattered.   It cannot go straight to the mark, because
it is aiming at no particular target.

As in *English Bards*, a large proportion of the satire is
placéd in prose notes.   The longest passage of satire in
verse is that directed at Jeffrey.   The lines:—

> "On shores of Euxine or Ægean sea,
>   My hate, untravelled, fondly turned to thee,"

show that Byron's rage at that critic was still smouldering.
Repeating the bombastic challenge uttered in the postscript to the second edition of *English Bards*, the satirist
taunts Jeffrey with disinclination or inability to reply to
the assault made upon him.   It is probable that the Scotch-
man never saw this passage in *Hints from Horace;* at any
rate he did not deign to answer Byron's abuse, and maintained a discreet silence during the period of the latter's
anger.

The lines on Southey reiterate in a commonplace fashion
what Byron had said before on the same subject, a long
prose note dwelling on the heaviness of Southey's epics,
particularly of *The Curse of Kehama* (1810), which had
recently appeared.   Another elaborate note is aimed at
the "cobbler-laureates," Bloomfield and Blackett, whom
Byron still mentions with contempt.   Scott and Bowles
receive some passing uncomplimentary remarks; Fitzgerald
is referred to once as "Fitz-scribble"; Wordsworth is
barely alluded to, and Coleridge is not spoken of at all.
The review of the drama is uninteresting and dull.   Byron
persists in his condemnation of the Opera on the ground of its
immorality, although, somewhat inconsistently, he defends
plays against the prudish censure of "Methodistic men."

An occasional line suggests a similar passage from other English satirists.   Thus Byron's couplet,

"Satiric rhyme first sprang from selfish spleen.
You doubt—see Dryden, Pope, St. Patrick's Dean,"

recalls the words of Cowper,

"But (I might instance in St. Patrick's Dean)
Too often rails to gratify his spleen."[1]

The reference to Pitt's skill in coining words may have been remembered from many jests on the subject in the *Rolliad* and the Works of Peter Pindar.   The scorn of "French flippancy and German sentiment" re-echoes the violent opposition of the *Anti-Jacobin* to the spread of foreign ideas.   A note on "the millennium of the black letter"[2] calls to mind the hatred of Mathias for antiquaries and searchers for old manuscripts[3] and another note[4] reinforces Gifford in abusing T. Vaughan, Esq., the "last of the Cruscanti."

The single striking feature of *Hints from Horace* is its summary of "Life's little tale," based upon a corresponding passage in the *Ars Poetica*, in which Byron describes graphically the career of a young nobleman under the Georges, from his "simple childhood's dawning days" to the time when "Age palsies every limb," and he sinks into his grave "crazed, querulous, forsaken, half-forgot."   Despite some obvious exaggerations and some traces of affected pessimism, the poet was undoubtedly drawing largely upon his own experience.   The tone of the lines is bitter, unrelieved by sympathy or humor, paralleled in Byron's work only in the *Inscription on the Monument of a Newfoundland Dog*.

The Curse of Minerva, composed at approximately the same time as *Hints from Horace*,—it is dated from the Capu-

[1] *Charity*, 420–500.   [2] *Poetry*, i., 396.
[3] *Pursuits of Literature*, page 93.   [4] *Poetry*, i., 444.

chin Convent at Athens, March 17, 1811—was actually printed in 1812, but not for public circulation. The first edition, probably unauthorized, was brought out in Philadelphia in 1815. Meanwhile the 54 introductory lines, beginning:—

> "Slow sinks, more lovely ere his race be run,
> Along Morea's hills the setting sun,"

had appeared in Canto III of the *Corsair* (1814). A fragmentary version of 111 lines, entitled *The Malediction of Minerva, or the Athenian Marble-Market*, signed "Steropes" and published in the *New Monthly Magazine* for April, 1815, was disowned by Byron as a "miserable and villanous copy."[1] The stanzas on Lord Elgin in *Childe Harold*[2] had already expressed Byron's condemnation of the conduct of that nobleman, and the poet doubtless believed that nothing was to be gained by again airing his indignation. Possibly, too, as Moore suggests,[3] a remonstrance from Lord Elgin or some of his relatives may have been an inducement to sacrifice a work which could add little to his reputation.

The Curse, unlike *Hints from Horace*, has the advantage of a definite and undivided aim. It is an exposure and denunciation of Lord Elgin, who, appointed in 1799 to the embassy from England at the Porte, had interested himself in the remains of Greek architecture and sculpture on the Acropolis and had secured the services of the Neapolitan painter, Lusieri, to sketch the ruins. In 1801 he obtained a firman from the Sultan allowing him to carry away "any pieces of stone with old inscriptions or figures thereon," and accepting this as a guaranty against molestation in his project, he at once proceeded, at his own expense, to dismantle the Parthenon and to ship the finest specimens to

[1] *Letters*, iii., 271.   [2] *Childe Harold*, II., 10–15.
[3] *Life of Byron*, ii., 145.

England. Although he left Turkey in 1803, the work continued through his agents until 1812. His collection, the
cost of accumulating which was estimated at 74,000 pounds,
was purchased by the nation for 35,000 pounds in 1816, and
now forms part of the so-called "Elgin Marbles" in the
British Museum.

Although opinions as to the propriety of Elgin's actions
differed widely at the time, it is now fairly well established
that his foresight prevented the ultimate destruction of the
statuary by war and the elements. Byron's conclusions,
formed on the spot where the operations were being carried
on, have, however, some justification. He felt that it was
the degradation of Greece at the hands of a foreign despoiler,
and he resented the intrusion as interference in the affairs
of a helpless people. In *English Bards* he had mentioned
Elgin, along with Aberdeen, as fond of "misshaped monu-
ments and maimed antiques," and had ridiculed him for
making his house a mart,

"For all the mutilated works of art."

When later he saw the havoc that had been caused at Athens,
his mood changed from raillery to seriousness, and he burst
out with fury at the man whom he considered a wanton
plunderer and at the nation which could tolerate his depredations. Under this stimulus he wrote the stanzas on
Elgin in *Childe Harold*, but his rage found a better outlet
in *The Curse of Minerva*. This satire contains only 312
lines, but it goes straight to its goal, with a directness and
a concentration which distinguish it above any of the other
early satires, even above *English Bards*, superior as that
poem is to it in more important respects.

The satire has a narrative basis, with a plot which is
simple and unified. The beautiful opening description of
an evening at Athens precedes, and accentuates by contrast,

the ensuing indictment by Minerva' of Elgin, the desecrator of all this loveliness.   The poet's reply to the accusing goddess disclaims any responsibility for the vandalism on England's part, and lays the blame on Scotland, Elgin's fatherland.   Minerva's answering curse and prophecy extend the scope of the satire beyond mere personal malice, and give it a broad application to England's policy as oppressor and devastator.   Her speech ends somewhat abruptly, and the poem closes.

Although Byron was, by his own admission, "half a Scot by birth, and bred a whole one,"[1] he joined, in *The Curse of Minerva*, the long line of satirists from the authors of *Eastward Ho!* to Cleveland with his grim couplet,

"Had Cain been Scot, God would have changed his doom;
    Not forced him wander but confined him home,"

and to Dr. Johnson, who have jeered at the Scotch and Scotland.   Byron's antipathy for his early home evidently developed from his quarrel with the Scotch reviewers. *English Bards* had contained scattered references to "Northern wolves" and to the "oat-fed phalanx" of the critic clan, and had alluded scornfully to the children of Dun-edin who "write for food—and feed because they write."   In *The Curse of Minerva*, a new occasion for dislike having arisen, the attack on the Scotch is more vicious and intolerant.   Many passages have their counterparts in portions of Churchill's *Prophecy of Famine* (1763), a pastoral in the form of a dialogue, with the motto, "Nos patriam fugimus," ingeniously applied to the Scotch in the translation,"We all get out of our country as fast as we can."   Churchill, who, it will be remembered, hated the Scotch critic, Smollett, as ferociously as Byron hated Jeffrey, had been aroused also by the growing influence of Bute and other Scotchmen at

[1] *Don Juan*, x. , 17.

the court of George III, and his poem, accordingly, became
a severe political invective, interspersed with vilification of
the Scotch climate and the Scotch people.   It is interesting
to compare Churchill's description of the barrenness and
dampness of Scotland with Byron's picture of that country
as "a land of meanness, sophistry, and mist."   The former
poet calls Scotchmen "Nature's bastards"; Byron refers
to Scotland as "that bastard land."   Both writers have
caustic lines on the shrewdness, importunity, and avarice
of the Scotch people, wherever they settle.   Although the
similarities between the satires warrant no deduction, there
is a possibility that Byron, who undoubtedly had read the
Prophecy of Famine, may have recollected certain passages
in a poem the spirit of which is very like his own.[1]

Basing his argument chiefly on the fact that a couplet of
Pope[2] is parodied in Byron's lines,

> "'Blest paper-credit!' who shall dare to sing?
> It clogs like lead Corruption's weary wing,"

Weiser has endeavored to prove that Byron borrowed something from Pope's *Epistle to Lord Bathurst*.   A verbal
comparison of the two passages in question fails to bring
out any striking resemblance.   Pope continues with a
comment on the ease with which paper money may be used
in bribery; Byron, after quoting Pope, does not touch on this
point, and his lines seem to be merely a passing quotation,
not closely connected with what comes before or after.   In
no other place in *The Curse of Minerva* are there phrases
which have even a remote likeness to the language of Pope's
Epistle.   On such grounds as Weiser advances it might be

---

[1] Churchill's poem ends with a prophecy from the Goddess of Famine
just as Byron's ends with Minerva's curse.

[2] "Blest paper-credit! last and best supply!
That lends Corruption lighter wings to fly!"
(*Epistle to Lord Bathurst, On the Use of Riches*, 40-41.)

shown that Byron, in *Beppo*, is imitating Cowper, because he quotes a line from that poet.

Byron's attack on Lord Elgin in *Childe Harold* had been animated by a love for Greece and a pity for her forlorn state among the nations, as well as by resentment of England's cold-blooded attitude in allowing such depredations. In the passage Byron had covered Elgin with abuse:—

> "Cold as the crags upon his native coast,
>   His mind as barren and his head as hard,
>   Is he whose head conceived, whose hand prepared,
>   Aught to displace Athena's poor remains."[1]

These lines were published in March, 1812. In 1813, James and Horace Smith, famous through their *Rejected Addresses*, appeared again as authors in *Horace in London*, a series of imitations of the first two books of the *Odes* of Horace. In this volume, Ode XV, *The Parthenon*, modelled fairly closely in plot on Horace's *Prophecy of Nereus*, treats of the controversy concerning Elgin. A clear reference to Byron in the poem makes it certain that the Smiths had read *Childe Harold* and that they concurred with his expressed disapproval of Elgin's conduct.

The Parthenon, owing perhaps to mere coincidence, perhaps to the possibility that the Smiths may have had access to *The Curse of Minerva* in manuscript, is in its outlines and especially in the general features of Minerva's curse, singularly like Byron's satire. The Smiths, following Horace, describe Elgin's ship as hastening homeward, laden with the "guilty prize." Suddenly Minerva rises, like Nereus, from the sea and, with the language of a prophet, pronounces a curse on the destroyer, predicting that Elgin will suffer misfortunes and go down through the ages remembered for his shamelessness. The poem, like Byron's, closes with Minerva speaking. Certain lines in *The Parthenon*:—

[1] *Childe Harold*, II., 12.

"Goth, Vandal, Moslem, had their flags unfurl'd
Around my still unviolated fane,
Two thousand summers had with dews impearl'd
Its marble heights nor left a mouldering stain;
'T was thine to ruin all that all had spared in vain,"[1]

epitomize a longer passage in *The Curse of Minerva*.[2] In
Childe Harold Byron had made no mention of the fact that
Elgin's marriage had been dissolved by act of Parliament
in 1818, but in *The Curse of Minerva* he made the goddess
allude to the domestic scandal. A similar passage is introduced into Minerva's prophecy in *The Parthenon*. These
resemblances in structure and sometimes in phrasing may,
of course, have occurred independently, or may have arisen
from the chance that Byron, as well as the Smiths, was
thinking of Horace's *Ode*. On the other hand, there is a
possibility that the Smiths, already familiar with the lines
on Elgin in *Childe Harold*, may have read *The Curse of
Minerva* in manuscript and have unconsciously reproduced
some of its features in their poem.

By a natural transition Minerva, in Byron's satire, leaves
Elgin and turns to England in the words,

"Hers were the deeds that taught her lawless son
To do what oft Britannia's self had done."

This introduces a survey of England's foreign affairs,
designed to expose that country's despotic policy towards
her weaker rivals and dependents. The goddess treats
briefly of England's treachery to Denmark in the battle of
Copenhagen, of the recent uprisings of the natives in India,
and of the misfortunes of the Peninsular War in Spain and
Portugal, and finally, touching upon domestic matters,

---

[1] *The Parthenon*, stanza 3.   [2] *The Curse of Minerva*, 95–116.

uncovers the distress and misery of the laboring classes in England and the inefficiency of the government in dealing with internal problems. She ends with a picture of the Furies waving their kindled brands above the distracted realm, while ascending fires shake their "red shadow o'er the startled Thames." Such a fate, says Minerva, and Byron with her, is deserved by a nation which had lit pyres "from Tagus to the Rhine."

This passage, commonplace enough in its style, is significant in that it shows Byron almost for the first time taking a keen and active interest in politics, and posing as an adverse critic of England's foreign policy. It was easy for the man who could condemn England's conduct towards Denmark and India to develop into an outspoken radical.

In neglecting and partly disowning *The Curse of Minerva*, Byron was probably acting with good judgment. It is assuredly unworthy of the author of *Childe Harold*. Only the opening passage is notable for its genuine poetry, and the satire, except in structure, is inferior to *English Bards*. It is equally true, however, that it is superior in most respects to *Hints from Horace* and *The Waltz*. *The Curse of Minerva*, with its narrative basis, is a variation from the other early classical satires; but it has the same elaborate machinery of notes, the same method of direct attack— although in this instance it is conveyed through the mouth of a third character—and the same extravagance and bitterness of tone. In managing the heroic couplet, Byron never surpassed his skill in *English Bards*. After 1811 his acquired ability to handle other measures withdrew his attention from the metre of Pope, with the result that his versification in the ensuing classical satires shows signs of deterioration and weakness. It is to this period of decline that *Hints from Horace* and *The Curse of Minerva* belong.

CHAPTER VI

DURING the seven years between the completion of *The Curse of Minerva* and the publication of *Beppo*, Byron's contributions to satire were, on the whole, sporadic, ephemeral, and unworthy of his genius. He composed in this period only one long formal satire, *The Waltz*, and that appeared anonymously, to be disowned by its author. The remaining satiric product may be divided into three groups: political epigrams and squibs, like *Windsor Poetics*, many of them printed in the newspapers, others sent in letters to friends; jocular and fragmentary *jeux d'esprit*, often, like *The Devil's Drive*, semi-political; and ironical and invective verses dealing with his domestic troubles, illustrated by *A Sketch*. Nearly all are timely impromptus, to few of which he gave careful revision. The period is plainly transitional, for it marks the gradual change in Byron's satiric method from the formal vituperation of *English Bards* to the colloquial raillery of *Beppo*. Little by little he forsakes the heroic couplet for other measures; more and more he diverges in practice from the principles of his masters, Pope and Gifford. As he grows more experienced and more mature, he tends to employ mockery as well as abuse, and in this development is to be seen an approach to the manner and spirit of *Don Juan*.

The causes for the comparative unproductivity in satire of this period in Byron's life are by no means difficult to discover. The years which followed his return from abroad saw his dramatic entrance into London society, his association with leaders in politics and literature, his engagement to Miss Milbanke and eventual marriage to her on January 2, 1815, and his separation from her in 1816. Before 1812 he had been a somewhat isolated author; now he was a prominent and much discussed personage, busy with duties and engagements. It is true that even in the midst of these exciting days he did not cease writing; but his interest had been turned to the verse romance, popularized in England by Scott, and his literary work resulted in *The Giaour* and the narrative poems which followed it in rapid succession. Engaged in so many pleasurable pursuits, the poet had small inclination for sustained effort, and contented himself with pouring forth, with astonishing facility and fluency, these melodramatic Eastern tales. Possibly, too, his circumstances were so fortunate up to 1816 that he did not resort instinctively, as he did later, to satire as a means of voicing his dissatisfaction with men and things. It was not until he had been driven from his native land by the condemnation of his countrymen that his satiric spirit became again a dominant mood.

To comprehend the development of Byron's political views, it is necessary to understand the conditions under which he formed them. After two previous attacks of insanity, George III became permanently demented in 1810, and the Regency Bill, making Prince George actual ruler of the nation, was passed on February 5, 1810. His well-known vicious propensities and illicit amours had made him unpopular, and when, on February 23, 1812, he first appeared in public as sovereign, he was coldly received. It had been generally supposed that with the power in his hands, he would reward the Whigs who had stood by him so faithfully through his many difficulties, but after vain efforts to organize a coalition ministry, he appointed Lord Liverpool as Prime Minister on June 9, 1812, and the Tories retained complete control over affairs of state. This action, equivalent to treachery, made the Regent a target for Whig abuse, and that party never ceased reviling the ruler who had been disloyal to their cause.

Byron at Cambridge had rather lukewarmly supported Whig doctrines, and when he took his seat in the House of Lords, he selected one of the neutral benches. Undoubtedly the attack upon him by the Whig *Edinburgh Review* inclined him to look askance on the party of which he was temperamentally a member; and it will be remembered that in *English Bards* he had assailed Lord Holland and other prominent Whigs. Once in London, however, he allied himself with the opposition, and soon became a regular visitor at Holland House. His three speeches in Parliament were in advocacy of liberal measures, the first, on February 27, 1812, being delivered in resistance to a bill instituting special penalties against the frame-breakers of Nottingham, and the second being a plea for Catholic emancipation. Scott's suggestion that Byron's liberalism was due "to the pleasure it afforded him as a vehicle of displaying his wit and satire against individuals in office" is not needed to explain the latter's preference for Whig policies, for the poet would have joined himself inevitably to the more progressive and more radical party. Although his political beliefs at this time were somewhat vague and occasionally inconsistent, he was by nature an individualist and an opponent of conservatism. His espousal of liberal views may, however, have been assisted by his intimacy with Moore, Leigh Hunt, and other radical writers.

In reply to Byron's attack on him in *English Bards*, Moore had sent the satirist a letter on January 1, 1810, preparatory to a challenge unless reparation were offered. Fortunately the note did not reach Byron until his landing in England, when the Irishman's wrath had cooled and he himself was in a repentant mood. A short correspondence led to the meeting of the two, with Campbell and Rogers, at the house of the latter in November, 1811, where the difference was amicably adjusted. On December 11th Byron invited Moore to visit him at Newstead, and though Moore found it impossible to accept, the poets soon became good friends.[1] It was not until the formation of this friendship that Byron began to take any active part in current politics; during the rest of his life, however, he was linked with Moore as a satirist on the Whig side and was, to a considerable extent, influenced by the latter's work.[2]

As we have seen, Moore had failed in his attempts at formal satire; but in 1812, shortly after his acquaintance with Byron began, he commenced his persistent and stinging gibes at the Regent and his coterie. On February 13, 1812, the Prince sent his notorious letter to the Duke of York, asking for Whig support, and Moore's admirable verse parody was soon in private circulation. This was one of the earliest, and certainly one of the most delightful, of the many brilliant satires with which Moore, for years, amused the town. In March, 1813, under the pen-name of "Thomas Brown, the Younger," he published *Intercepted Letters; or the Two-penny Postbag*, in which he borrowed the structure of the anonymous *Groans of the Talents* by pretending to have discovered a number of letters from various celebrated personages. Moore's letters, eight in all, are in rapid anapestic and octosyllabic metres, and are unusually bright and piquant, full of allusions to the scandalous gossip of

[1] Byron expressed his esteem for his new friend in his Journal, December 10, 1813:—"I have just had the kindest letter from Moore. I *do* think that man is the best-hearted, the only *hearted* being I ever encountered; and then, his talents are equal to his feelings" (*Letters*, ii., 371).

[2] See Byron's impromptu lines to Moore in a letter of May 19, 1812, in which he says, speaking of a projected visit to Hunt in prison:—
"Pray Phœbus at length our political malice
May not get us lodgings within the same palace."
(*Letters*, ii., 204–209.)

court life. Although Moore continued his satires in numerous verses of a similar type, he never excelled this first success.

In March, 1812, Byron joined Moore in assailing the Regent. In the Whig *Morning Chronicle* for March 7th was printed a short epigram without a signature, called *A Sympathetic Address to a Young Lady*. The lines read as follows:—

> "Weep, daughter of a Royal line,
> A Sire's disgrace, a realm's decay;
> Ah! happy! if each tear of thine
> Could wash a father's fault away!
> Weep—for thy tears are Virtue's tears—
> Auspicious to these suffering isles;
> And be each drop, in future years,
> Repaid thee by thy people's smiles."

The poem refers to an incident which had taken place at Carlton House a few days before, when the Princess Charlotte had burst into tears on learning that her royal father was intending to desert his Whig adherents. No one, apparently, suspected that Byron was the author; but in the second edition of the *Corsair* (February, 1814) the verses appeared as *Lines to a Lady Weeping*, publicly avowed by him. His acknowledgment brought upon him a storm of abuse from Tory papers—the *Courier*, the *Morning Post*, and the *Sun*—and a discussion ensued entirely out of proportion to the merit of the epigram which had excited it.[1] "How odd," wrote Byron to Murray, "that *eight lines* should have given birth, I really think, to *eight thousand*."[2] It is probable that no single production of Byron's aroused more hostile comment at the time of its appearance.

Byron's attitude towards the Regent at this period

---

[1] See *Letters*, ii., 463–492 (Appendix vii.).   [2] *Letters*, iii., 61.

exposes him to a charge of double-dealing.   In June, 1812,
three months after the composition of the epigram, he met
the Prince at a ball in an interview in which the two men
conversed on Scott and his poetry.   In relating the talk to
Scott, Byron mentions that the Regent's opinions were
conveyed "with a tone and taste which gave me a very high
idea of his abilities and accomplishments, which I had
hitherto considered as confined to *manners*, certainly superior to those of any living *gentleman.*"[1]   It is probable that
Byron was a little flattered by the Prince's condescension;
but his own tactlessness in acknowledging his epigram prevented any further intercourse, and he subsequently became
the Regent's open enemy.

   Jeaffreson suggests that Byron's avowal of the *Lines to a
Lady Weeping* may have been hastened by his sympathy
with Leigh Hunt,[2] who, with his brother, John Hunt, had
been tried for a libel on the Regent printed in their *Examiner* for March 12, 1812, and sentenced to two years' imprisonment and a fine of 500 pounds.   Byron saw a kindred
spirit in Hunt, and, after meeting him in prison in May,
1813, became his close friend.   Hunt, on his part, stood by
Byron in his *Examiner* at the time of the latter's separation
from his wife, and dedicated to him his *Rimini* (1816).
Byron, after the unfortunate circumstances connected with
The Liberal, modified his lofty opinion of Hunt; but in 1813
the latter was, to Moore and Byron, simply a martyr to
liberal principles, a man who had been unjustly persecuted
and condemned.[3]   There is, however, no evidence to justify
Jeaffreson's conclusion.

   In his satire on "the first gentleman of Europe," Byron

---

[1] *Letters*, ii., 134.

[2] *The Real Lord Byron*, ii., 51.

[3] On December 2, 1813, Byron wrote Hunt:—"I have a thorough
esteem for that independence of spirit which you have maintained with
sterling talent, and at the expense of some suffering" (*Letters*, ii., 296).

was both less prolific and more savage than Moore. His satiric spirit, as usual, was stimulated by particular incidents which offered an opportunity for timely comment. It had been ascertained accidentally that Charles I had been buried in the vault with Henry VIII; and on April 1, 1813, the Regent was present at the opening of the coffins containing the ashes of the two sovereigns. This episode Byron made the theme of two short satires: *Windsor Poetics*, circulated in manuscript among his friends, but not printed until 1819; and the lines *On a Royal Visit to the Vaults*, published first in 1904. The point in both poems is the same— that George combines the vices of his two predecessors:

"Charles to his people, Henry to his wife,—
In him the double tyrant starts to life."

In mentioning *Windsor Poetics*, the better of the two poems, to Moore, Byron confessed, with some discernment: "It is too *farouche;* but, truth to say, my satires are not very playful."[1]

The vindictive seriousness of Byron's satire, as contrasted with Moore's playfulness, is nowhere better shown than in the *Condolatory Address to Sarah, Countess of Jersey*, printed without his permission in the *Champion*, July 31, 1814, after it had been sent to the lady herself in a letter of May 29. Once a favorite of the Regent's, Lady Jersey had incurred his dislike by her kindness to the deserted Princess of Wales, with the result that the Prince returned to Mrs. Mee, the painter, a miniature of the Countess, and announced his intention of ignoring her. Byron, who had been more than once the guest of Lady Jersey, saw a chance to strike a blow in her defense by assailing the Regent, and his lines on that ruler are scathing:

[1] *Letters*, iii., 58.

> "If he, that Vain Old Man, whom truth admits
> Heir of his father's crown, and of his wits,
> If his corrupted eye and withered heart,
> Could with thy gentle image bear to part;
> That tasteless shame be *his*, and ours the grief
> To gaze on Beauty's band without its chief."

In satire of this sort there is nothing sportive or delicate; it is sheer invective of the kind which Byron had used on Clarke and was to employ against Castlereagh.

Byron never became reconciled to the Regent, not even when, as George IV, the latter ascended the throne. Indeed what is probably the poet's most bitter estimate of his sovereign was sent in a letter to Moore on September 17, 1821— the lines now entitled *The Irish Avatar.* Queen Caroline had died on August 7, 1821, shortly after the failure of her husband to secure a divorce, and not over a week later, the king was feasted with regal pomp at Dublin by the servile Irish office-holders. The combination of circumstances was fit material for satire, and Byron spoke out in stanzas that ring with rage and contempt:—

> "Shout, drink, feast, and flatter! Oh! Erin, how low
> Wert thou sunk by misfortune and tyranny, till
> Thy welcome of tyrants had plunged thee below
> The depth of thy deep in a deeper gulf still."

The satire in this poem is as spontaneous and sincere as any Byron ever wrote; it is passionate, convincing, laden with noble scorn. The two methods of irony and invective are admirably mingled, without a trace of humor.

We have already noticed some early poems in which Byron had evinced a liking for uncommon rhymes. In the humorous *Farewell to Malta*, written May 26, 1811, and printed in 1816, he employed octosyllabics, with such rhymes as: yawn sirs—dancers, fault's in—waltzing, prate is—gratis. *The Devil's Drive*, an irregular and amorphous fragment, broken off on December 9, 1813, also contains some extraordinary rhymes; but it deserves attention especially because it anticipates, to some extent, the thought and manner of *Don Juan*. It is styled a sequel to *The Devil's Walk*, a fanciful ballad composed by Southey and Coleridge in 1799, but attributed by Byron to Porson, the great Cambridge scholar. Byron's poem, a rambling and discursive satire, is crammed with allusions to current events, prophetic of the views which he was to advocate during the remainder of his career. It describes a night visit of the Devil to his favorites on earth, in the course of which he pauses to survey the battle-field of Leipzig, and then, passing on to England, investigates a Methodist chapel, the Houses of Parliament, a royal ball, and other supposed resorts of his disciples. Byron's portrayal of the horrors of war is probably his first satiric expression of what was to become a frequent theme in his later work, and especially in *Don Juan*. As the Devil gazes down with glee at the bloody plain of Leipzig, the satirist remarks:

"Not often on earth had he seen such a sight,
　　Nor his work done half so well:
For the field ran so red with the blood of the dead,
　　That it blushed like the waves of Hell!"[1]

The visit of the Devil to Parliament, with the poet's comment on the spectacle there, is reminiscent of some sections of the *Rolliad*. The satire concludes with some caustic characterizations of Tory statesmen, some observations on the immorality of round dancing, and a picture of sixty scribbling reviewers, brewing damnation for authors.

[1] Byron's attitude towards war recalls the sardonic passage on the same subject in *Gulliver's Travels*, Part IV.

The significant feature of *The Devil's Drive* is the mocking spirit which animates the poem. Although the humor is sometimes clumsy and cheap, and the style formless and crude, the underlying tone is no longer ferocious, and the satire is no longer mere invective. The work is practically the only satire of Byron's before *Beppo* in which are mingled the cool scorn, the bizarre wit, and the grotesque realism which were to be blended in *Don Juan*. The poem, too, is proof that by 1814, at least, Byron was firmly fixed in most of his political opinions. He had shown his dislike for Castlereagh and the Regent; he had expressed himself as opposed to all war and bloodshed, except in a righteous cause; and he had become an advanced liberal thinker, ready to oppose all unprogressive measures.

After the publication of the *Corsair* in January, 1814, Byron announced his intention of quitting poetry.[1] His resolution, however, was short-lived, for on April 10th he wrote Murray that he had just finished an "ode on the fall of Napoleon."[2] Byron had, from the first, been interested in the career of Napoleon, with whom he felt, apparently, an instinctive sympathy. The poet's expressed judgments of the Emperor seem, however, to indicate several changes in sentiment. In *Childe Harold* he had called him "Gaul's Vulture," and had spoken of "one bloated chief's unwholesome reign"; in his Journal for November 17, 1813, he said: "He (Napoleon) has been a *Héros de Roman* of mine—on the Continent—I don't want him here."[3] The *Ode to Napoleon Buonaparte*, composed in a single day after the news of the abdication of Fontainebleau, is a severe attack on the fallen Emperor, in which Byron, reproaching him for not having committed suicide, terms him "ill-minded man," "Dark Spirit," and "throneless homicide," ending with an uncomplimentary contrast between him and Washington. Nevertheless, when the report of Waterloo reached him,

[1] *Letters*, iii., 64.   [2] *Letters*, iii., 66.   [3] *Letters*, ii., 324.

Byron cried: "I am damned sorry for it." In three poems written shortly after—*Napoleon's Farewell, Lines from the French*, and *An Ode from the French*—he shows a kind of admiration for the Corsican. Finally came the splendid stanzas on Napoleon in *Childe Harold*, III,[1] ending with the personal reference, implying that Byron's own faults and virtues were those of the French emperor and exile.

The one long classical satire during this period is *The Waltz*, which has to do primarily with society. On October 18, 1812, Byron wrote Murray: "I have a poem on Waltzing for you, of which I make you a present; but it must be anonymous. It is in the old style of *English Bards, and Scotch Reviewers.*"[2] The satire was printed in the spring of 1813, but was so coldly received that Byron, on April 21, 1813, begged Murray to deny the report that he was the author of "a certain malicious publication on Waltzing."[3] The whole affair leaves Byron under the suspicion of duplicity.

The poem was published with a motto from the Aeneid:

"Qualis in Eurotæ ripis, aut per juga Cynthi,
 Exercet Diana choros,"

and with a prefatory letter from "Horace Hornem, Esq.," the professed author. This imaginary personage is a country gentleman of a Midland county, who has married a middle-aged Maid of Honor. During a winter in town with his wife's relative, the Countess of Waltzaway, Hornem sees his spouse at a ball, waltzing with an hussar, and, after several vain attempts to master the new dance himself, composes the satire in its honor, "with the aid of William Fitzgerald, Esq.—and a few hints from Dr. Busby." In the poem, however, Byron apparently makes no effort to fit the language or style to this fictitious figure.

[1] *Childe Harold*, III., 36–52.   [2] *Letters*, ii., 176.   [3] *Letters*, ii., 202.

Although the waltz, brought originally from Germany, was, in 1812, steadily winning its way to acceptance by the more fashionable element of society, its introduction was still meeting with opposition from many quarters. Byron, as censor of the Italian Opera and of Little's *Poems*, was certainly not inconsistent in disapproving of the foreign dance on the ground of its immodesty. Doubtless, too, his own lameness, which prevented him from participating in the amusement, had some influence on his attitude. He had denounced the dance in *English Bards* in the line,

"Now in loose waltz the thin-clad daughters leap,"

and in Section 25 of *The Devil's Drive*, he had made the Devil's fairest disciples waltzers, and had quoted Satan's words:

"Should I introduce these revels among my younger devils,
    They would all turn perfectly carnal."

Byron's declaration that *The Waltz* is in the style of *English Bards* is not altogether exact, for though the metre of the two satires is the same and the same machinery of prose notes is used in both poems, the first-named work has a kind of jocularity which distinguishes it from the more severe earlier production. *The Waltz*, moreover, has some features of the mock-heroic, although the conventional structure of that *genre* is not made conspicuous. Thus it begins with an apostrophe to "Terpsichore, Muse of the many-twinkling feet," and later, in true heroic manner, the author exclaims,

"O muse of Motion! say
    How first to Albion found thy Waltz her way?"

The personification of "Waltz," carried out for a time in such phrases as "Nimble Nymph," "Imperial Waltz,"

"Endearing Waltz," and "Voluptuous Waltz," is, however, often disregarded or forgotten. She is described as a lovely stranger, "borne on the breath of Hyperborean gales," from Hamburg to England, and welcomed there by the "daughters of the land." At this point the mock-heroic element ceases to be noticeable, and the rest of the poem is devoted to an exposure of the iniquity which the new dance had brought into English high society.

It is in *The Waltz* that Byron for the first time manifests the ability to deal with political questions in a lighter vein, in a manner something like that of Moore. He alludes, for instance, to the Regent's well-known preference for ladies of a mature age:

"And thou, my Prince! whose sovereign taste and will
It is to love the lovely beldames still."

This topic Moore touched upon frequently, particularly in *Intercepted Letters*, II, from Major M'Mahon, the Regent's parasite and pander, and in *The Fudge Family in Paris*, Letter X, in which Biddy Fudge says,

"The Regent loves none but old women you know."

A note to line 162 of *The Waltz* has a joking reference to the Regent's whiskers, an adornment which had excited Moore's merriment, especially in his "rejected drama," *The Book*, appended to Letter VII of *Intercepted Letters*. The fact that the dance is an importation from Germany allows Byron to sum up ironically what England owes to that country:

"A dozen dukes, some kings, a Queen—and Waltz."

The body of the satire is occupied with a description of the dance itself, given in lines which are too often more prurient and suggestive than the waltz could possibly have been.   Byron is here surely not at his best, and his coarseness is not extenuated by his alleged moral purpose.   Weiser's judgment that *The Waltz* is the ripest of Byron's youthful poems will, to most critics, seem unwarranted. There is barely a line of the satire which is either witty or epigrammatic; the style is low and the language is cheap in tone; the versification is lifeless and dull.   The one thing for which it is to be noted is the spirit of mockery sometimes displayed, and the tendency to jest rather than to inveigh.

The competition for a suitable dedicatory address for the reopening of Drury Lane Theatre in 1812,[1] memorable as the occasion for the skilful parodies contained in the *Rejected Addresses*[2] of James and Horace Smith, led Byron also to compose a rather extraordinary satire.   The genuine address of Dr. Busby (1755–1838) had been rejected, along with those of the other competitors; but on October 14th, two or three evenings after the formal opening of the theatre, Busby's son endeavored to recite his father's poem from one of the boxes, and nearly started a riot.   Byron thereupon wrote a *Parenthetical Address, by Dr. Plagiary*, which was printed in the *Morning Chronicle* for October 23, 1812. This satire, which Byron called "a parody of a peculiar kind," is noteworthy only in that it selects lines and phrases

[1] Byron himself was asked to compete, but resolved not to risk his reputation in such a contest.   Although 112 poems were submitted, all were adjudged unsatisfactory, and Byron was eventually requested by Lord Holland to save the situation.   His verses were recited on October 10, 1812, but met with small commendation.

[2] This little volume, published in 1812, after having been refused by Murray and others, proved an overwhelming success.   Byron was delighted with *Cui Bono?* a clever imitation of the gloomy and mournful portions of *Childe Harold*, in the same stanzaic form.   Among the other writers parodied were Wordsworth, Crabbe, Moore, Coleridge, and Lewis.   Byron said:—"I think the *Rejected Addresses* by far the best thing of the kind since the *Rolliad*" (*Letters*, ii., 177).

from Busby's address, and connecting them by satiric comments, manages to make the original seem ridiculous.

The story of Byron's love affairs between 1812 and 1817 has been so often related that any presentation of the details here is unnecessary, especially since in only one case did his amours lead him to satire. According to Medwin, Lady Caroline Lamb, the fickle and incorrigible lady who so violently sought Byron for a lover, called one day at the poet's apartments, and finding him away, wrote in a volume of *Vathek* the words "Remember me." When Byron discovered the warning, he added to it two stanzas of burning invective, concluding,

> "Remember thee! Aye, doubt it not.
>   Thy husband too shall think of thee;
> By neither shalt thou be forgot,
>   Thou false to him, thou fiend to me!"

Several theories have been advanced to explain the causes and results of Byron's unfortunate marriage, but the main facts seem to be simple enough. In 1813 he proposed to Miss Milbanke, a cousin of Lady Caroline Lamb's by marriage, and was refused. The intimacy of the two continued, however, and a second offer, made in 1814, was accepted. The wedding, which took place on January 2, 1815, was accompanied by some inauspicious omens, but the honeymoon, spent at Halnaby, was apparently happy. Byron's financial circumstances were straitened, and, on his return to London, he was pursued by creditors. He himself was irritable, unsuited for a quiet domestic life, and Lady Byron was probably over-puritanical. At any rate, whoever may have been the more at fault, his wife, soon after the opening of 1816, left him, took steps to have his mental condition examined, and later demanded a separation. In this crisis of his life, public opinion sided with Lady Byron, and the poet became a social outcast.[1]   The deed of separation was signed on April 22, 1816, and on the 25th of the same month, Byron left England forever.

During the arrangements for the separation Byron showed no resentment towards his wife.   Indeed he wrote Moore on March 8, 1816:—"I do not believe—that there ever was a better, or even a brighter, a kinder, or a more amiable and agreeable being than Lady Byron."[2]   His wrath fell heavily, however, on Mrs. Clermont, Lady Byron's old governess, who had come to stay with her mistress when the trouble began.   On her Byron laid the responsibility for the events which followed.   He thought her a spy on his actions, accused her of having broken open his desk in order to read his private papers, and considered her an impudent meddler.   As he signed the deed of separation, he muttered, "This is Mrs. Clermont's work."   His full rage against her burst out in *A Sketch*, finished March 29, 1816, and published, through some one's indiscretion, in the Tory *Champion* for April 14th.   Fifty copies of this satire were printed for private circulation, with Byron's poem *Fare Thee Well*, addressed to his wife.   The appearance of these verses in the newspapers started a violent controversy in the daily press, carried out on party lines.

A Sketch, containing 104 lines in heroic couplets, is a coarse and scurrilous attack on Mrs. Clermont, beginning with a short account of her life,

"Born in the garret, in the kitchen bred,
    Promoted thence to deck her mistress' head,"

and closing with a terrible imprecation,

---

[1] Byron himself said of this period:—"I felt that, if what was whispered and murmured was true, I was unfit for England; if false, England was unfit for me" (*Reply to Blackwood's, Letters*, iv., 479).

[2] *Letters*, iii., 272.

"May the strong curse of crush'd affections light
Back on thy bosom with reflected blight!
And make thee, in thy leprosy of mind,
As loathsome to thyself as to mankind!"

Perhaps no more savage satire was ever levelled at a woman; it is even more venomous than Pope's assault on Lady Montagu in what Mr. Birrell calls "the most brutal lines ever written by man of woman." Murray wrote Byron, after showing the satire to Rogers, Canning, and Frere:— "They have all seen and admired the lines; they agree that you have produced nothing better; that satire is your forte; and so in each class as you choose to adopt it."[1] These men, however, were active supporters of Byron, and their praise seems extravagant. Whatever his provocation may have been—and it was probably great—Byron did not enhance his fame by this barbarous tirade.

In the very midst of his anger the poet pauses in the poem to pay his wife a tribute and to assert his love for her; but not long after he turned to assail Lady Byron herself. Indeed he is said to have attached an epigram to the deed of separation,

"A year ago you swore, fond she!
'To love, to honour,' and so forth:
Such was the vow you pledged to me,
And here 's exactly what 't is worth."

In September, 1816, when he was in Switzerland, he wrote the *Lines on Hearing that Lady Byron Was Ill*, in which he fairly gloats over her in her sickness. No one can mistake the meaning of the line,

"I have had many foes, but none like thee,"

or of the charge,

[1] *Letters*, iii., 278.

"Of thy virtues didst thou make a vice,
Trafficking with them in a purpose cold,
For present anger and for future gold."

These stanzas, however, were not printed until 1832. In the meantime Byron had continued the attack on his wife in *Childe Harold*, III, 117, and IV, 130–138, in *Don Juan*, and in an occasional short epigram sent to friends in England. There can be no doubt that as the years went by and his attempts at reconciliation were thwarted, he grew thoroughly embittered against her.

Byron's habits of thought were so frequently satirical that it was natural for him to introduce satire even into poems which were obviously of a different character. In his preface to *Childe Harold* he announced his intention of following Beattie in giving full rein to his inclination, and being "either droll or pathetic, descriptive or sentimental, tender or satirical" as the mood came to him. In that poem the moralizing and didactic elements often closely approach satire, and there are some passages of genuine invective, a few of which have already been indicated.

In the first canto a visit to Cintra leads Byron into an indictment of the Convention of Cintra (1808), signed by Kellerman and Wellesley, by the terms of which the French troops in Portugal were permitted to evacuate with artillery, cavalry, and equipment. This agreement was regarded by the home officials as equivalent to treason, and the men responsible were subjected to some rigorous criticism. Byron took the popular side of the question in saying,

"Ever since that martial synod met,
Brittannia sickens, Cintra, at thy name."[1]

This patriotic mood seems, however, to have been a passing one. In after years he was not inclined to take the part

[1] *Childe Harold*, I., 26.

of his country. Of a different sort are the stanzas on a London Sunday[1] which, in Moore's opinion, disfigure the poem. Canto I has also some satiric animadversions upon women, notably the lines,

"Maidens, like moths, are ever caught by glare,
And Mammon wins his way where Seraphs might despair."[2]

In the final version of the first two cantos some stanzas of a satiric tone were omitted, among them lines on Frere, Carr, and Wellesley in Canto I, and passages on Elgin, Hope, Geil, and the "gentle Dilettanti" in Canto II.

A few ephemeral verses of this period still remain unnoticed: an occasional epistle in rhyme to Moore or Murray; four brief squibs on Lord Thurlow's poetry; and several unimportant epigrams on trivial subjects. No one of them is significant as literature, and they may well be passed by without comment.

In a last glance at Byron's satiric production from 1811 to 1818 we perceive that, with the single exception of *Hints from Horace*, an avowed imitation, his work was directed towards definite ends. He was little given to vague denunciation; on the contrary, in touch as he was with current events and a keen observer of what was going on around him, he aimed, in his satire, at specific evils and follies. It is interesting, too, that most of his work after his return from abroad was journalistic and transitory, hastily conceived and carelessly composed. At the same time there are signs of a change in spirit. Though he still continues to burst out into invective on provocation, he is beginning to recognize the value of humor and mockery. More and more he is employing new metrical forms, and neglecting the heroic couplet for freer and more varied measures.

When Byron left England in 1816, he had been taught

[1] *Childe Harold*, I., 69–70.   [2] *Childe Harold*, I., 9.

much by experience and had acquired some maturity of judgment.   To some extent, though not entirely, he had outgrown the affectation and morbid pessimism of his boy-hood.   In a stern school he had learned many lessons, and, as a result, his satire from the time of his voluntary exile until his death displays a different spirit.   When at last he discovered an artistic form and style in which to embody it, it showed a decided gain in merit and originality over *English Bards*, which, in 1817, was still the best satire he had written.

CHAPTER VII

SHORTLY after the momentous year 1816, an extraordinary development took place in the form and spirit of Byron's satiric work in verse. Up to this date, as we have seen, his satires of any literary value had followed, as a rule, the general plan and manner used by the authors of such typical productions as the *Dunciad*, the *Rosciad*, and the *Baviad*. In some ephemeral verses, it is true, he had shown signs of breaking away from the English classical tradition; but few, if any, of these unimportant occasional poems had been printed in book form. They had appeared in newspapers or in letters to correspondents, and Byron himself would have made no claim for their permanence. His published satires, then, had deviated little from the standard set by Pope and Gifford, a fact all the more remarkable because his work in the other branches of literature in which he had distinguished himself had revealed a wide discrepancy between his utterances as a critic and his practice as a poet. The enthusiastic and often extravagant eulogist of Pope had been the author of the romantic *Childe Harold* and *The Giaour*. In one field of letters, however, Byron had preserved some consistency; before 1818, considered as a satirist, he must be classed as one of the numerous disciples of the great Augustan.

The publication of *Beppo*, February 28, 1818, may serve roughly to denote the visible turning-point between the old era and the new one to come. It is significant that this poem is written, not in the characteristically English heroic couplet, but in the thoroughly foreign ottava rima. Responsive to an altered and agreeable environment, Byron found in Italy and its literature an inspiration which affected him even more profoundly than it had Goethe only a few decades before. The results of this influence, shown to some extent in his dramas though more decidedly in his satires, justify terming the years from 1817 until his death his Italian period. A mere mention of its contribution to satire indicates its importance: it produced *Beppo*, *The Vision of Judgment*, and *Don Juan*. Of these poems, *Beppo* is, strictly speaking, a satiric novella; *The Vision of Judgment* is a travesty; and *Don Juan* is an "epic satire." They are, however, all three closely related: first, in that, unlike most of the earlier satires, they are narrative in method; second, in that they are infused with what we may call, for want of a better phrase, the Italian spirit. What this spirit is we may well leave for future discussion. It is enough here to point out that it is characterized by a kind of playfulness, half gayety and half mockery, often tinged with irony and reflecting a cynical tolerance, and that it adopts a style informal and colloquial, in which the satirist unbends to his readers and feigns to let them into his confidence. The bare outlining of these features alone proves how far Byron departed from the usually serious, dignified, and formal satire of Pope and Gifford.

It would, of course, be erroneous to assume that Byron, before he first touched Italian soil in 1816, was unfamiliar with the language. If, as Moore says, he had read little of it up to 1807, he still must have gained some acquaintance with it on his early travels, for on January 14, 1811, he wrote his mother from Athens:—"Being tolerably master of the Italian and Modern Greek languages—I can order and discourse more than enough for a reasonable man."[1] In a

[1] *Letters*, i., 308.

letter of August 24, 1811, he used Italian words,[1] and in 1812 he criticized with much intelligence the "Italian rhymes" of W. R. Spencer.[2] There are several references in his Diary to his study of Italian writers.[3] In his library, sold in 1816 to satisfy his creditors, were many Italian books; indeed Fuhrman computes that by that date he had gone through Dante, Petrarch, Boccaccio, Boiardo, Bandello, Ariosto, Alfieri, Monti, and Goldoni, besides many minor historians, essayists, and poets.[4] Finally when he actually set foot in Italy, he was able to assure Murray:—"As for Italian, I am fluent enough."[5] Nothing up to this time, however, had induced him to become an imitator of the Italians. Although he had commended Hunt's *Rimini* for having two excellent features, "originality and Italianism," he had, apparently, no idea of emulating Hunt in seeking for a stimulus from Italian sources.

In mid-October, 1816, Byron arrived in Italy from Switzerland, making his first halt at Milan. From then on until he set out for Greece on July 23, 1823, he was a continuous dweller in the peninsula, settling for a time at and near Venice, in the meanwhile making an excursion to Florence and Rome, going later to Ravenna, and at last residing at Pisa and Genoa. The interesting details of his life in these places are sufficiently well known through his own letters and the records given to the world by Hunt, Medwin, the Countess of Blessington, Trelawney, Moore, and others. His reputation as the author of *Childe Harold* served as a means of introduction to men of letters; his noble birth procured him admission into social circles; and naturally he acquired an intimate knowledge of Italian customs, as well as a wide acquaintance with the literature of the coun-

[1] *Letters*, ii., 5.   [2] See *Letters*, ii., 413 (Appendix i.).
[3] *Letters*, ii., 379; ii, 403.
[4] See Fuhrman's *Die Belesenheit des jungen Byron*, Berlin, 1903.
[5] *Letters*, iii., 19.

try, both mediæval and modern. He engaged in several
liaisons in Venice, and in 1819 became the accepted *cicisbeo*
of the Countess Guiccioli. ⟨ By aiding the secret organiza-
tion of the Carbonari, he enrolled himself in the struggle
for Italian independence and made himself an object of
suspicion to the police. It is no wonder that he wrote to
Moore in 1820:—"I suspect I know a thing or two of Italy—
I have lived in the heart of their houses, in parts of Italy
freshest and least influenced by strangers—have seen and
become (*pars magna fui*) a portion of their hopes, and fears,
and passions."[1] The immediate consequences of this assimi-
lation may be recognized in *Beppo*, composed in 1817,
which, slight and inconsiderable though it seems, is nevertheless the prelude to the fuller voice of *Don Juan*, the
product of Byron's ripest genius.

The problem is to determine, as far as it is possible, in
what way and to what extent Byron is indebted to Italy
and Italian writers in *Beppo*, *The Vision of Judgment*, and
Don Juan. The process of arriving at a satisfactory answer
to these queries cannot be an easy one, because it so often
necessitates dealing with qualities of style which are somewhat intangible. We may set aside at once any supposition
that Byron stole habitually from the Italian satirists by
translating their phrases or transferring their ideas, unac-
knowledged, to his own pages. He was rarely a plagiarist
in the sense that he conveyed the words of others bodily into
his own stanzas, and when, as in sections of *Don Juan*, he
paraphrased the prose of historians, he frankly admitted
his obligation. But his creative impulse was likely to be
affected by any book which had recently aroused his admiration. Moore, who knew the operations of Byron's
mind as no one else did, said:—"There are few of his poems
that might not . . . be traced to the strong impulse given
to his imagination by the perusal of some work that had

[1] *Letters*, v., 70.

just before interested him."[1] Obviously, when a particular
poem was composed under such inspiration, we shall find
it difficult to measure the extent of Byron's dependence
upon the book which offered him a stimulus. Now and
then, it is true, there aɪe passages in his satires which recall
at once similar lines in Italian writers, and occasionally we
find him using a trick of theirs which it seems improbable
he could have learned elsewhere: in such cases the relationship is clear enough. On the other hand, we may feel
convinced that Byron drew from the Italian satirists something of their general tone, and yet be unable to clarify
our reasons for this belief or to frame them into an effective
argument. Of such a sort, indeed, is much of the influence
which Pulci, Berni, and Casti had on Byron. It is vague
and evasive, but it undoubtedly exists. Perhaps at bottom
it is little more than the habit of thinking in a peculiar way
or of surveying objects from an unusual point of view. But
whatever is the basis of this satiric manner, it influenced
Byron's work, and made his later satires almost unique in
English.

It is in *Beppo*, as has been said, that this new mood first
has full expression. Yet, curiously enough, we are at once
forced into the paradox that Byron may have been taught
something of the Italian spirit in *Beppo* through the medium
of an English poem, to which he explicitly turns our attention. In 1817 a book was published by Murray with the
odd title, *Prospectus and Specimen of an Intended National
Work, by William and Robert Whistlecraft, of Stowmarket, in
Suffolk, Harness and Collar Makers, Intended to Comprise the
Most Interesting Particulars Relating to King Arthur and his
Round Table.* The volume contained only two short cantos
in ottava rima, the whole making up, with the eleven
stanzas of introduction, 99 stanzas, exactly the length of
Beppo. Early in 1818 two more cantos were added, and

[1] *Life of Byron*, iv., 237.

in the same year the entire poem was printed as *The Monks, and the Giants*. Although no author's signature was attached, credit was rightfully bestowed upon John Hookham Frere (1769–1846), already mentioned as a brilliant contributor to the poetry of the *Anti-Jacobin*.[1] Like Mathias, Roscoe, Rose, and others among his contemporaries, Frere had been an assiduous student of Italian, and had read extensively in the Italian romantic and burlesque poets from Pulci to Casti. It was doubtless interest in this literature that led him to the composition of *The Monks, and the Giants*, for which work he borrowed from the Italians their octave stanza, an occasional episode, and as much of their manner as his nature could absorb.[2]

Byron's first mention of *Beppo* occurs in a letter of October 12, 1817, to Murray:—"I have written a poem (of 84 octave stanzas), humourous, in or after the excellent manner of Mr. Whistlecraft (whom I take to be Frere), on a Venetian anecdote which amused me."[3] On October 23d he repeats this assertion:—"Mr. Whistlecraft has no greater admirer than myself. I have written a story in 89 stanzas, in imitation of him, called *Beppo*."[4] Although the definiteness of these statements is unquestionable, it is, neverthe-

[1] Frere was well known in 1817 as a prominent London wit. His career as a diplomat, which apparently promised him high preferment, had been cut short by some unlucky transactions leading to his being held partly responsible for the failure of the Peninsular campaign, and he had been recalled in 1809 from his position as envoy to Ferdinand VII. of Spain. The incident drew upon him Byron's lines on "blundering Frere" in some expunged stanzas of *Childe Harold*, I. Piqued by the action of the government and constitutionally inclined to inactivity, Frere had since led an indolent and self-indulgent existence as scholar and clubman.

[2] Dr. Eichler finds that Frere drew something from Aristophanes and Cervantes, but more from Pulci, Berni, and Casti. For Frere's indebtedness to the Italians, see Eichler's *Frere*, 115.

[3] *Letters*, iv., 172.   [4] *Letters*, iv., 176.

less, essential to ascertain just how literally we are to accept Byron's confession that *Beppo* is "in the excellent manner of Mr. Whistlecraft."

The problem has been discussed in detail by Albert Eichler in his treatise, *John Hookham Frere, Sein Leben und seine Werke, Sein Einfluss auf Lord Byron* (1905), and his conclusions are, in many respects, trustworthy. After comparing *Beppo* with Frere's poem, Dr. Eichler maintains that Byron's inspiration may be traced to *The Monks, and the Giants*, and makes the following assertion regarding the sources of Byron's work:—"Die Italien duerfen wir als Quellen hiebei mit Recht nach des Dichters eigenen Auesserungen und auch aus zeitlichen Gruenden ausschliessen." This statement, which is certainly stronger than the evidence warrants, may be controverted on two grounds: first, that, in spite of some superficial resemblances between the two poems, there is much in *Beppo* that Byron could not have gained from Frere, indeed which he could have learned only from a close study of the Italian poets; secondly, that Byron actually knew the work of Casti well at the time when he composed *Beppo*.

The likeness in stanza form and Byron's own acknowledgment of his model have, in all probability, been somewhat over-emphasized. So much do the two works differ in plot that there is no single case in which Byron could have adopted a situation or an incident from Frere. The story of *The Monks, and the Giants* is told by an imaginary personage, Robert Whistlecraft, just as *The Waltz* is supposed to have been composed by the fictitious "Horace Hornem, Esq.," and the language of the poem is fitted to the station and education of this figure, who is thoroughly British and entirely Frere's creation. The poem itself, fragmentary and amorphous even in its final state, is a jumble of poorly organized themes. Beginning in Canto I with a description of Arthur's court and of his three valorous knights, Lance-

lot, Tristram, and Gawain, it proceeds to treat in Canto II
of an attack of the banded Arthurian chivalry on the castle
of the Giants, a race who resemble, in some respects, the
giants in Pulci's *Morgante Maggiore*. At this point the
knights disappear from the story, Arthur being mentioned
only once during the rest of the tale, and Frere, imitating
in part the first canto of the *Morgante Maggiore*, takes a
monastery for his scene and a siege of the religious brethren
by the Giants for his main action. Friar John's quarrel
with the Tintinabularians, his enforced leadership after
the death of the venerable abbot, the assault of the Giants,
the successful defence of the Monks, and the eventual
retreat of the assailing party:—these are the significant
incidents in the second half of a work which obviously
depends little on the unity of its plot.

Beppo is also a narrative, founded on a rather unim-
pressive anecdote. The merchant, Beppo, departed on a
trading trip, fails to return to his wife, Laura, and she,
thinking him dead, consoles herself with a Count for her
lover. After some years, Beppo comes back, to meet his
wife and her cavalier at a ball. She is reconciled to her
husband, the Count becomes Beppo's friend, and the story
ends. Since these main features of the plot differ so widely
from the incidents in *The Monks, and the Giants*, we are
forced to seek, therefore, for similarities in manner and
style between the two poems.

Unquestionably the fact that Frere's work was written
in ottava rima[1] did affect Byron. It is true that the latter

---

[1] While it is undisputed that the ottava rima is a native Italian
stanza, its origin has never been satisfactorily determined. That it
was a common measure before the time of Boccaccio is easily demon-
strable; but it is equally probable that he, in his *Teseide*, was the earliest
writer to employ it consciously for literary purposes. With him it
assumed the form which it was to preserve for centuries: eight endecasyllabic lines, rhyming ababcc. In Pulci's *Morgante Maggiore*

poet had selected the octave stanza for his *Epistle to Augusta*, composed near Geneva in 1816, before he had entered Italy and before Frere's poem had come to his attention; but the *Epistle* had been serious and romantic, without a touch of humor or of satire. Byron had also been familiar with the use of the octave stanza in Ariosto's *Orlando Furioso*, and, as we shall see, in Casti's *Novelle*. But of its employment in English for humorous purposes there had been few

---

it became freer and less dignified, without losing any of its essential characteristics. Pulci made ottava rima the standard measure for the Italian romantic epic and burlesque, and it was used by men differing so greatly in nature and motive as Boiardo, Berni, Tasso, Marino, Tassoni, Forteguerri, and Casti. To the Italian language, rich in double and triple rhymes, it is especially well suited; and its elasticity is proved by its effective employment in both the lofty epic of Tasso and the vulgar verse of Casti.

In English the borrowed ottava rima has had strange vicissitudes. Transferred to our literature, along with other Italian metrical forms, by Wyatt and Surrey, it was managed by them crudely, but still with some success. At least nineteen short poems by Wyatt are in this stanza. A typical illustration of its state at this period may be examined in Surrey's *To His Mistresse*. In Elizabethan days the octave had a sporadic popularity. Although Spenser made choice of his own invented stanza for his *Faerie Queen*, he tried ottava rima in *Virgil's Gnat*. Daniel in *The Civille Warres* and Drayton in *The Barrons' Warres* associated it with tedium and dulness. It was, of course, natural that Fairfax, in his fine version of Tasso, should adopt the stanza of his original; and Harington translated Ariosto in the same measure, giving it, probably for the first time in English, a little of the burlesque tone which was typical of the Italians. Milton, in the epilogue to *Lycidas*, used the octave with reserved stateliness; while Gay, in *Mr. Pope's Welcome from Greece*, made it a vehicle for quiet merriment.

During the eighteenth century the predominance of the heroic couplet hindered the spread of exotic verse forms—and the octave was still exotic. In 1812, William Tennant (1786–1846), an obscure Scotch schoolmaster, revived it in his burlesque epic, *Anster Fair*, modifying the structure by changing the last line to an alexandrine. Then came Merivale, Byron, Rose, Procter, and Keats, who settled the measure as a standard form in modern English literature.

examples, and Byron made no reference to any such experiments by English poets.

In managing the octave, Frere had resorted to a somewhat free and loose versification, diversified by frequent run-on lines and many novel rhymes. Probably this unconstrained metrical structure appealed greatly to Byron; but it must be remembered that since 1811 he had been avoiding the heroic couplet and practising in some less restricted measures. In *Childe Harold* he had used a true stanzaic form, occasionally with humorous effect. He had also, even in his first published volume, shown facility in the rhyming of extraordinary words and combinations of syllables, an art in which he had as guides Butler, Swift, and Moore, all of whom were more skilful than Frere. Granting that Frere did suggest to Byron the possibility of making the octave a colloquial stanza, we cannot escape the conclusion that the latter went beyond his model. For one thing, he was less careful about accuracy in rhyming. Eichler, after a detailed examination of *The Monks, and the Giants* and *Beppo*, estimates that in the former poem only one rhyme out of thirty is humorously inexact, in the latter, one out of six. Frere's entire work, more than double the length of *Beppo*, has only eleven examples of "two-word rhymes," while *Beppo* has fifty-one. Eichler's tables show conclusively that Byron employed for rhymes many more foreign words and proper names than Frere, and that he discovered more odd combinations of English words. In addition he utilized the enjambement in a more daring fashion. Certainly, in nearly every respect, Byron was more lax in his versification than Frere had been in his.[1]

Another uncommon feature of *The Monks, and the Giants* is its adoption of a vocabulary drawn from the language of every-day life. Whistlecraft, the imaginary author, is, we

[1] For a detailed comparison of the versification of *Beppo* with that of *The Monks, and the Giants*, see Eichler's *Frere*, 170–184.

are led to understand, a rather talkative bourgeois. In fitting his diction to this middle-class artisan, Frere introduced many expressions which seem unpoetic, and consciously avoiding any effort at elevated speech, aimed at a kind of colloquial talk, illustrated in such contractions as, "I 'll" and " I 've" and slang phrases like "play the deuce." The vigor and picturesqueness of this conversational style impressed Byron and doubtless had some influence in leading him, in *Beppo*, to sink into street-jargon, well adapted to the tone of his poem. To some extent, as Eichler indicates, this informal diction coaxed him away from the correctness of Pope, and enabled him to give freer rein to his shifting moods.

The fictitious Whistlecraft has a habit, corresponding somewhat to a peculiarity of the Italian burlesque poets, of digressing from the main thread of the story in order to gossip about himself or his opinions. The first lines in the poem,

> "I 've often wished that I might write a book
> Such as all English people might peruse,"[1]

set a conversational key. The introduction of eleven stanzas is devoted to a prefatory monologue, and in the body of the work there are digressions in the same vein, never long continued, and each in the nature of a brief aside to the reader. Sometimes they are merely interpolations having reference to the narrator's method:

> "We must take care in our poetic cruise,
> And never hold a single tack too long."[2]

In other cases, they are comments suggested by a turn in the

[1] *The Monks, and the Giants*, Introduction, 1.
[2] *The Monks, and the Giants* I., 9.

plot. With this feature of *The Monks, and the Giants*
Byron was, of course, familiar through his reading in one
or more of the Italian writers from whom Frere had partly
borrowed it, and when he adopted it in *Beppo*, he reverted
to them rather than to the Englishman.   The element of
digression does not become conspicuous in Frere's poem
until the last two cantos, which could not have influenced
Byron in *Beppo*.[1] Again Frere, who was deficient in
aggressiveness, had not wished to employ the digression
as a means of introducing personal satire.   Since he himself
remained anonymous and did not pretend to make his
poem a polemic, he refused to utilize these opportunities
for advancing his particular whims or prejudices.   Byron,
however, seeing the possibilities latent in the discursive
method and recalling its importance in Italian satire, used
it for the promulgation of his ideas, interesting himself
more in his chat with the reader than he did in the story.
In *Beppo* he constantly wanders from the tale to pursue
varied lines of thought, returning to the plot more from a
sense of duty than from desire.[2]   In these talks with his

---

[1] Dr. Eichler has neglected to notice the important fact that at the
time of the composition of *Beppo*, Byron could have been familiar with
only the first two cantos of *The Monks, and the Giants*.   A brief comparison of dates will establish this point.   Cantos I. and II. of Frere's
poem were published in 1817; *Beppo*, written in the autumn of 1817
(*Letters*, iv., 172), was sent to Murray on January 19, 1818 (*Letters*, iv.,
193), and given out for sale on February 28 of the same year.   Not until
later in 1818 were the last two cantos of Frere's work printed, and the
full edition of four cantos came out some months later.   On July 17,
1818, Byron wrote Murray, "I shall be glad of Whistlecraft," referring
doubtless to the newly issued complete edition of *The Monks, and the
Giants*.

[2] Only 36 of the 99 stanzas in *Beppo* are devoted entirely to the plot.
The greater portion of the poem is occupied with digressions upon many
subjects, containing some personal satire, some comment on political
and literary topics, and much discursive chat upon social life and morals.
The plot serves only as a frame for the satire.

audience, full of satiric references to English manners and morals, and tinctured with mocking observations on his contemporaries, Byron follows Casti rather than Frere.

These resemblances in outward form seem to indicate along what lines Byron was affected by Frere's poem. The differences in spirit and motive between the two men are indeed striking. *The Monks, and the Giants* belongs unmistakably to the burlesque division of satire: it is, said Frere, "the burlesque of ordinary rude uninstructed common sense—the treatment of lofty and serious subjects by a thoroughly common, but not necessarily low-minded man— a Suffolk harness maker."[1] The poem is, for the most part, satiric only in an indirect and impersonal way, and there is in it very little straightforward destructive criticism, like that in *English Bards*. Nor is there any underlying bitterness or indignation; it would be futile to seek, in these verses so marked by mildness, geniality, and urbanity, for any purpose beyond that of amusing, in a quiet way, a cultivated circle of friends. Even in the gossipy introduction there are few allusions to current events, and if, as has been claimed, the knights of the Round Table are intended to represent prominent living personages, no one uninitiated could have discovered the secret. Frere himself said of it: "Most people who read it at the time it was published would not take the work in a merely humorous sense; they would imagine it was some political satire, and went on hunting for a political meaning." When we recall that Byron spoke of *Beppo* as "being full of political allusions,"[2] we comprehend the gap which separates the two works.

The real divergence between the poems—and it is a wide one—is due, as Eichler intimates, to the characters of the authors. Whistlecraft's words:—

[1] See *Memoir of Frere*, i., 166. [2] *Letters*, iv., 193.

"I 'm strongly for the present state of things:
I look for no reform or innovation,"[1]

summarize Frere's conservative position. He was a Tory,
and Byron was a radical. Frere approached his theme from
the standpoint of a scholar; Byron, from that of a man of
the world. The former, actuated by antiquarian interest,
built up a background in a fabulous age and took his
characters from legend; the latter, urged by a desire for
vividness and reality, laid his action in a city which he
knew well and placed his men and women in modern times.
The Tristram and Gawain of *The Monks, and the Giants*
are puppets and abstractions; Laura and the Count, on
the other hand, are drawn from life and consequently seem
to throb with warmth and passion. There are no women
in Frere's poem who receive more than cursory notice; in
Beppo the central figure is a woman, and the atmosphere
vibrates with love and intrigue. One result of these contrasts is that *The Monks, and the Giants*, unexceptionable in
morality, lacks charm and is somewhat chastely cold; while
Beppo, sensuous and frequently sensual, is never dull. It
is obvious, then, that the two poems, however much they
may resemble each other superficially, have fundamentally
little in common.

What, then, did Byron take from Frere to substantiate
his assertion that *Beppo* is "in the excellent manner of Mr.
Whistlecraft"? He may have learned from him some lessons in the management of the English octave, particularly
as employed in humorous verse; he probably accepted a
hint concerning the use of the language of every-day life;
and he may have drawn a suggestion as to the value of the
colloquial and discursive method. In each of these features,
as we have seen, he surpassed his predecessor. Specifically
in the matter of direct satire he could have gained little

[1] *The Monks, and the Giants*, III., 59.

from Frere, for the latter was but a feeble satirist. Eichler
sums up the logical conclusion: "Die *Monks and Giants*,
eine amuesante Burleske, haben in *Beppo* eine moralische
Satire gezeugt."[1] The same idea is brought out by the
anonymous writer of a *Letter to Lord Byron, by John Bull*
(1820), in comparing Frere's poem with *Don Juan;*— "Mr.
Frere writes elegantly, playfully, very like a gentleman,
and a scholar, and a respectable man, and his poem never
sold, nor ever will sell. Your *Don Juan*, again, is written
strongly, lasciviously, fiercely, laughingly—and accordingly
the *Don* sells, and will sell, until the end of time." In
habits of mind and in temperament, Byron was more akin
to Frere's Italian masters than he was to Frere himself;
and therefore, in his knowledge of Casti, later of Berni and
Pulci, and possibly of Ariosto, Forteguerri, Tassoni, and
Buratti, we shall be more likely to discover the sources of
the spirit of *Beppo* and *Don Juan*.

   Of these men it is probable that Giambattista Casti
(1721–1804) is the nearest congener of Byron in the satiric
field. The fact that his work has never been subjected to
careful scrutiny by critics in either Italy or England
accounts possibly for the general ignoring of Casti as an
inspiration for Byron's Italian satires.[2] In spite of Eichler's
positive statement that the Italians "aus zeitlichen Gruenden" may be neglected as sources for Byron's work,[3] it is
certain that Byron had read Casti before he wrote *Beppo;*
for in 1816 he said to Major Gordon, referring to a copy of
Casti's *Novelle* which the latter had presented to him at
Brussels: "I cannot tell you what a treat your gift of
Casti has been to me: I have got him almost by heart. I

---

[1] Eichler's *Frere*, 184.

[2] In his *Studies in Poetry and Criticism* (London, 1905), Churton Collins pointed out Byron's indebtedness to Casti, but mentioned only
Casti's *Novelle*. See Collins's volume, pp. 96–98.

[3] Eichler's *Frere*, 163.

had read his *Animali Parlanti*, but I think these *Novelle* much better. I long to go to Venice to see the manners so admirably described."[1] Not until March 25, 1818, does he mention Berni, and he does not refer to Pulci until November, 1819. There is, then, presumptive evidence for maintaining that Byron, coming in 1816 or before in contact with the work of Casti, found in him some inspiration for the satiric method of *Beppo*, a method somewhat modified in *Don Juan* after a perusal of Berni and Pulci.

The *Novelle*, praised so highly by Byron, consist of forty-eight tales in ottava rima, printed together in 1804, although at least eighteen had been completed by 1778. Their author, a sort, of itinerant rhymester,[2] had acquired notoriety through his attacks on the reigning sovereigns of Europe, especially on Catharine II, whom he had assailed in *Il Poema Tartaro*, a realistic and venomous portrayal of Russian society and politics, containing a violent assault on the Empress. Although Casti's poems are now forgotten, their vogue during his lifetime was considerable. His greatest work, *Gli Animali Parlanti*, was translated into several languages, including

---

[1] *Letters*, iv., 217.

[2] Born in 1721 in Italy, Casti had been a precocious student at the seminary of Montefiascone, where he became Professor of Literature at the age of sixteen. In 1764 he moved, with the musician, Guarducci, to Florence, where he was created Poeta di Corte by the Grand Duke Leopold. Here he came to the attention of Joseph II., who invited him to Vienna and bestowed upon him several posts of honor. A lucky friendship with Count Kaunitz enabled him to visit most of the capitals of Europe in company with that Prime Minister's son, and he gained in this way an inside knowledge of court life in several countries. In 1778 he took up his residence in St. Petersburg, where Catharine II. received him cordially. Later he returned to Vienna and was crowned Court Poet by the Emperor Leopold. The attraction of the French Revolution drew him to Paris in 1796, where he lived until his death, February 16, 1804.

English, and Casti, as an apostle of revolt, was recognized as energetic and dangerous. His coarseness and vulgarity, however, combined with his slovenly verse structure and his neglect of art, prevented him from reaching a high position as a poet, and his literary importance was thus only temporary, occasioned principally by the popular interest in his timely satiric allusions. He, like Byron, was at heart a rebel, and in his own uncultivated way, he anticipated the spirit of the English poet. Indeed it is curious how often the two pursue the same general plan of attack on their respective ages.

The *Novelle Amorose* are verse tales of the type which Boccaccio, and after him, Bandello, Straparola, and their imitators, had made popular in prose. Dealing in a laughing and lenient fashion with the indiscretions of gallants, usually monks and priests, they are marred by grossness and indecency in plot and language. The cynical immorality of the stories has subjected Casti to much unfavorable criticism. Foscolo, his countryman, speaks of him as "spitting his venom at virtue and religion, as the sole expedient by which he can palliate his own immorality."[1] However, the coarse tone of the *Novelle* is hardly unique with Casti; he is merely adhering to the standard of the earlier prose novelists.

The likeness between *Beppo*, which is an English novella in verse, and some of Casti's *Novelle*, is one in manner and spirit rather than in plot and style.[2] Byron's story, taken

[1] *Quarterly Review*, April, 1819.

[2] Churton Collins, however, makes the statement that "*Don Juan* is full of reminiscences of the *Novelle*," and points out definite parallelisms between Novella IV., *La Diavolessa*, and the plot of *Don Juan*. He adds: "To Casti, then, undoubtedly belongs the honour of having suggested and furnished Byron with a model for *Don Juan*." (*Studies in Poetry and Criticism*, pp. 97-98.) It seems probable, however, that Byron took even more from *Il Poema Tartaro* than he did from the

as it was from an episode with which he had met in his own
experience, has no exact parallel in Casti's collection, but
his method of handling it is not unlike that followed by the
Italian in treating of themes not greatly dissimilar. Choos-
ing practically at random among the *Novelle*—for Casti's
plan was much the same in all—we may discover certain
peculiarities which have their counterparts in *Beppo*.
Novella IX, *Lo Spirito*, has, like *Beppo*, a humorous introduction, in which the narrator, speaking, like Byron, in the
first person, analyzes what is meant by "spirit" in man or
woman. He then proceeds with the adventure of the Lady
Amalia and her two lovers, describing each of the three in a
rather clever character sketch, not unlike the pictures
which Byron gives of Laura and the Count. The rival
suitors pursue different tactics in their struggles to win the
lady's favors and in dwelling on their actions, Casti often
pauses to indulge in a chuckling aside to the reader, never so
long continued as Byron's digressions, but in very much the
same vein. Finally one of the wooers meets with success,
and the tale concludes with a bantering moral.

Doubtless this summary of *Lo Spirito* fails to bring out
any convincing parallelisms between it and *Beppo;* and it
must be granted at once that the alleged relationship is
somewhat elusive. But there are some features common to
the two poems: an easy-going tolerance towards gallantry
and the social vices; a pretence of taking the reader into
the author's confidence; a general lack of formality and
rigidity in stanza structure; and a witty and burlesque
manner of turning phrases. Although one or two of these
characteristics had appeared singly in Byron's work before
1818, they had appeared in conjunction in no poem of his
previous to *Beppo*, with the possible exception of *The*

Novelle. Casti's *Gli Animali Parlanti* and *Il Poema Tartaro* are not
mentioned in Collins's study.

Devil's Drive, which was not in ottava rima. Obviously he could not have learned the secret of this new mood from Frere. Thus, when we consider that until Byron's acquaintance with Casti's work, this specific quality of mockery had not existed in his satire, we have reason for thinking that he was indebted to some extent to the Italian poet. Somehow the English writer, once a pretended defender of clean morals, began to take a tolerant attitude towards lapses from virtue; he changed from formal and dignified discourse to a style easy and colloquial; and he partly abandoned savage invective for scornful and ironic mockery. In *Beppo* we realize the full purport of the transformation which had been taking place in Byron's satiric mood ever since his return from Greece. Credit for this development must be given partly to Moore and partly to Frere; but it must be assigned even more to Casti, who first put Byron in touch directly with the Italian burlesque spirit.

If only the *Novelle* were considered, however, Byron's obligation to Casti would be confined chiefly to *Beppo*, for in his tales the Italian seldom leaves his theme, as Byron does in *Don Juan*, to assail individuals or institutions. He touches lightly on the weaknesses of human nature, on the frailties and illicit indulgences of full-blooded men and women, but he is swayed by no impelling purpose, and he wants the fundamental seriousness of the genuine satirist. Byron, on the other hand, in *Beppo*, and still more in *Don Juan*, never quite forgot the vituperative vigor which he had shown in *English Bards*.

But before he had seen the *Novelle*, Byron had read *Gli Animali Parlanti*, a mammoth work which, in its scope, in its antipathies, and in its manner, has some likeness to *Don Juan*. Published first in Paris in 1802, it was pirated in a London edition a year later, and before long had been translated into several languages. An English version in a greatly abridged paraphrase appeared in 1816 under the

title *The Court of Beasts,* in seven cantos, without the trans-
lator's name.[1]   The same volume, with revisions and addi-
tions, was reprinted in 1819 as *The Court and Parliament of
Beasts,*—freely translated, by Wm. St. Rose.

The Italian poem in three parts and twenty-six cantos
is written, not, as has been often taken for granted, in the
ottava rima, but in the less common sesta rima, a stanza
of six endecasyllabic lines, rhyming ababcc.   As its title
suggests, it is a beast epic, an elaboration of the fables
of Æsop and La Fontaine; but the allegory veils deliberate
and continuous satire.   In his prose preface, Casti explains
his object as being the presentation, with talking animals
as actors, of "un quadro generale delle costumanze, delle
opinioni, e dei pregiudizi dal pubblico adottati, riguardo al
governo, all' amministrazione ed alla politica degli Stati,
come delle passioni dominanti di coloro, che in certe emi-
nenti e pubbliche situazioni collocati si trovano, colorandolo
con tinte forti, ed alquanto caricate, le quali facilmente
ne relevino l'expressione—un quadro in somma della cosa,
e non delle persone."   Casti, then, planned a comprehensive satire on his own age, and despite his assertion that his
poem is "a picture of things, and not of persons," his real
object was, like Byron's, to "play upon the surface of
humanity."

The actual plot of *Gli Animali Parlanti* may be briefly
told.   The animals gather to organize a scheme of government, and, deciding on an hereditary monarchy, choose the
lion for their king.   At his death, a regency, headed by the
lioness, is established for his son, and conspiracy and corruption develop.   The dog, the first Prime Minister, is
superseded by the wolf, and becomes a rebel.   Civil war
ensues, and when, at length, all the conflicting parties unite

[1] To this work Byron refers in a letter to Murray, March 25, 1818:
"Rose's *Animali* I never saw till a few days ago,—they are excellent."
(*Letters,* iv., 217.)

for a conference, they are destroyed by a terrible storm. This, of course, is the barest outline of the story; the framework is filled out by argument and criticism by the various protagonists, many of whom, notably the dog, the horse, and the bear, represent political factions, conservative, moderate, and progressive. No small amount of satire lies in the actions and speeches of the beasts, who are intended to represent different types of humanity; their court is a mirror of the courts of western Europe, and the abuses which pervade it are those which Casti had seen on his travels. The animals are, in all save external appearances, like men.

Not enough of a reformer to evolve remedies, Casti was, nevertheless, alert in detecting faults in the inert institutions of his time and daring in his methods of assailing them. His poem, thus, is a hostile picture of politics and society in the Europe of the latter half of the eighteenth century, painted by a man who had studied his subject from a cosmopolitan standpoint. *Gli Animali Parlanti* is a radical document, designed to expose the flaws in existing systems. Even fads and foibles are not beneath its notice. It jeers at the academies so popular in Italy in Casti's youth, especially the notorious Accademia dell' Arcadia[1]; it makes sport of pedants and antiquaries[2]; it scorns literary and political sycophants[3]; it is bitter against theological quibbles, against monks,[4] and against superstitious practices.[5] Throughout it all runs Casti's hatred of despotism, and his dislike of hypocrisy and cant. It is not, indeed, unfair to Byron to declare that the scope of *Gli Animali Parlanti* is, in some respects, as broad and comprehensive as that of *Don Juan*.

It is interesting, as far as the material of Casti's poem is concerned, to notice that Casti is an advocate of what were

[1] *Gli Animali Parlanti*, VII., 6 ff. [2] *Ibid.*, III., 37.
[3] *Ibid.*, III., 32. [4] *Ibid.*, XX., 69. [5] *Ibid.*, XIV., 47; XVII., 36, 56.

to be some of Byron's pet theories.   For both men liberty
is a favorite watchword.   The horse, who seems to be spokes-
man for Casti himself, cries out,

"Noi d'ogni giogo pria liberi, e sciolti,"[1]

an assertion exactly in the spirit of Byron's words,

"I wish men to be free
    As much from mobs as kings—from you as me."[2]

A similar mood led them both to lay an emphasis on the
seamy and gruesome side of war, and to condemn it as
unnecessary and degrading.   Casti, after picturing all the
horrors of a battle-field, exclaims,

"Crudelissime bestie!   O bestie nate
    Per lo sterminio della vostra spezie."[3]

This is in the same tone as Byron's remark about the
futility of war:

"Oh, glorious laurel! since for one sole leaf
    Of thine imaginary deathless tree,
    Of blood and tears must flow the unending sea."[4]

Again and again in the two poems we meet with marked
coincidences in the manifestations of the revolt of the two
poets against the laws and customs of their respective
periods.

Don Juan, moreover, has many of the peculiar methods
which, partly the product of tradition in Italian burlesque
poetry, and occasionally the idiosyncrasies of Casti himself,

---

[1] *Gli Animali Parlanti*, I., 52.   [2] *Don Juan*, X., 25.
[3] *Gli Animali Parlanti*, XVIII., 33.   [4] *Don Juan* VII., 68.

are used regularly in *Gli Animali Parlanti*. Casti, for instance, protests continually in humorous fashion that he is dealing only with facts:

> "Poeta son io, non son causidico,
> E mio difetto è sol d'esser veridico."[1]

His unfailing insistence on this point gives his repeated professions an air of stock conventionality. Byron also employs this mocking manner of calling attention to the verisimilitude of his own work:

> "My muse by no means deals in fiction;
> She gathers a repertory of facts."[2]

More significant, perhaps, is the colloquial tone which Casti habitually adopts towards his readers, turning to them constantly to speak about himself, his plans, and his difficulties, sometimes to apologize, sometimes to make a confession:—

> "M'attengo a ciò che tocco, a ciò che vedo,
> Ne mi diverto a far castella in aria."[3]

This sort of intimate gossip is also characteristic of *Don Juan;* indeed Byron has elucidated his theory of procedure:

> "I rattle on exactly as I'd talk
> With anybody in a ride or walk."[4]

At the end of cantos this affectation of taking the public into confidence often becomes in *Gli Animali Parlanti* a

[1] *Gli Animali Parlanti*, IV., 13.
[2] *Don Juan*, XIV., 13. See also *Gli Animali Parlanti*, X., 1; XVIII., 32, and *Don Juan*, VII., 26, 41; VIII., 124.
[3] *Gli Animali Parlanti*, IV., 73.
[4] *Don Juan*, XV., 19. See also *Gli Animali Parlanti*, III., 95; VII., 38; *Don Juan*, VI., 8; VIII., 89; *The Vision of Judgment*, 34.

kind of sham humility, coupled usually with the poet's
promise to return another day, if encouraged. Thus Casti
closes a canto in this fashion:

> "Ma spossatello omai mi sento e roco,
> Ne in grado più proseguire il canto,
> Permettetemi dunque, almen per poco,
> Ch'io prenda fiato, e mi riposi alquanto.
> Che poi, qualor vi piaccia, io sarò pronto
> A riprendere il fil del mio racconto."[1]

There is space for quoting only one of several similar endings
from *Don Juan:*

> "But, for the present, gentle reader! and
> Still gentler purchaser! the Bard—that 's I—
> Must, with your permission, shake you by the hand,
> And so—'your humble servant, and Good-bye!'"[2]

These asides recall the personal paragraphs and short essays
which Fielding, and after him, Thackeray, were accustomed
to insert in their novels. Their importance in *Don Juan*
cannot be overestimated, for, as it will be necessary to
emphasize later, the satiric element in that poem is brought
out chiefly through these digressions, in which the author
gives free vent to his personality. Some traces of this
method had appeared even in the first two cantos of *Childe
Harold*[3]*;* and, to some degree, it had been utilized in several
of Byron's short verse epistles to friends. However the

---

[1] *Gli Animali Parlanti*, IV., 107.

[2] *Don Juan*, I., 231. See also *Gli Animali Parlanti*, XX., 126, and *Don
Juan*, IV., 117; V., 159; VI., 120; VII., 35; IX., 85; XV., 98.

[3] In *Childe Harold* the digression had been used, not for satire, but
for personal reminiscences, eulogy, and philosophical meditation; see
Canto I., 91–92, with its tribute to Wingfield, and Canto I., 93, with its
promise of another canto to come.

discursive style is not common in the poet's work before *Beppo*, and after that, at least in his satires, it comes to be conspicuous. Even Frere, familiar as he was with the Italians, did not realize the full value of the digression until he wrote the last two cantos of *The Monks and the Giants*, and, moreover, he never used it as an instrument for satire. It is, therefore, reasonable to suppose that Byron found a pattern for his procedure in the burlesque writers themselves and particularly in Casti. There are, however, some variations in Byron's employment of this device. He extended the colloquial aside until it verged almost into a prolonged monologue or satirical sermon; and whereas Casti, in *Gli Animali Parlanti*, seldom made use of the digression as an opportunity for personal satire, Byron improved the chance to speak out directly, in the first person, against his enemies. Casti advanced his destructive criticism largely through his narrative, by allusion, insinuation, and irony, in a manner quite indirect, keeping himself, as far as open satire was concerned, very much in the background. In *Don Juan*, on the contrary, as the poem lengthened into the later cantos, Byron tended more and more to neglect the plot and to reveal himself as a commentator on life.

In many respects, Casti's third poem, *Il Poema Tartaro*, which has never been mentioned in connection with Byron and which was never referred to by the English poet, is even more closely akin than *Gli Animali Parlanti* to *Don Juan*. It is possible that it may have offered a suggestion for a portion of the plot of *Don Juan*—the episode of Catharine II. It shows Casti speaking, for once, directly against great personages, bestowing upon them fictitious titles, but not at any pains to conceal the significance of his allusions. As *Il Poema Tartaro* is little known, it is essential to dwell somewhat upon its plot and general character.

The poem, which is made up of twelve cantos in ottava rima, treats mainly of the Russia of the Empress Catharine

II. Most of the important actors are historical figures,
disguised under pseudonyms: thus Catharine is called
Cattuna or Turrachina; Potemkin, her famous minister, is
Toto; and Joseph II, who receives his share of adulation, is
Orenzebbe.   No one of these characters is drawn with any
effort at secrecy; indeed, in most editions, a complete key is
provided.

In its chief features the narrative element of *Il Poema
Tartaro* is not unlike that of some sections of *Don Juan*.
The hero, a wandering Irishman, Tomasso Scardassale, like
Juan a child of pleasure and fortune unembarrassed by moral
convictions, joins a pilgrimage to the Holy Land.   Eventually he is captured by the infidels, falls into the hands of
the Caliph of Bagdad, and while a prisoner at his court,
engages in a liaison with Zelmira, a member of the harem.
An appointment to the office of Chief Eunuch having been
forced upon him, he flees with his inamorata and, after
some escapades, arrives at St. Petersburg, where he has the
good luck to please the Empress.   Soon, without any manifest reluctance on his part, he occupies the position of
official favorite, is loaded with money and honors, and
becomes, for a time, the second highest personage in the
realm.   After various incidents, including a rebellion
against the empress suppressed only with difficulty, and
visits of many contemporary monarchs to the capital,
Potemkin, Catharine's former lover, jealous of Tomasso's
rise to power, succeeds in bringing about his downfall, and
the discarded Irishman, suffering the usual penalty of the
Empress's caprices, is exiled to a far corner of Russia.   At
this point, Casti's poem, becoming prophetic, diverges
entirely from history.   There is an uprising led by the
Grand Duke; Catharine and Potemkin are seized and ban-
ished; and the Grand Duke is declared emperor.   Somewhat dramatically the poet describes the meeting between
the dethroned Catharine and Tomasso.   Finally the latter,

recalled to St. Petersburg, dies in the arms of his earlier love, Zelmira, and is buried with elaborate ceremony.

The Catharine II episode in *Don Juan* begins with Canto IX, 42, and ends with Canto X, 48. That there is a superficial resemblance between the adventures of the two heroes, Tomasso and Juan, is sufficiently obvious. Both are modern picaresque knights at the sport of circumstances. Each comes to St. Petersburg from Turkey, bringing with him a Turkish girl; each is installed as a favorite at the court and attains, at one bound, nobility and riches; each falls from his lofty state, and is sent away. It is evident, of course, that Byron in no sense borrowed from Casti's plot as he did from other writers in his description of the shipwreck. However, since Casti's poem is probably the only one of the period dealing with the court of Catharine II, and since Byron was well acquainted with the other two long works of the Italian, there are grounds for surmising that he took *Il Poema Tartaro*, in its general scheme, as a model for a part of *Don Juan*.

This supposition is strengthened by some resemblances in details between the two poems. Catharine II is portrayed by both authors in much the same way. Casti says of her that,

> "Per uso e per natura
> Ne' servigi d'amor troppo esigea,"[1]

and Byron echoes precisely the same idea:

> "She could repay each amatory look you lent
> With interest, and, in turn, was wont with rigor
> To exact of Cupid's bills the full amount
> At sight, nor would permit you to discount."[2]

She is generous to her favorites: Casti makes her confess,

[1] *Il Poema Tartaro*, II., 8.   [2] *Don Juan*, IX., 62.

> "Amare e premiar l'amato ogetto
> Sole è per me felicita e diletto,"[1]

And Byron refers particularly to her Kindness:

> "Love had made Catharine make each lover's fortune."[2]

Tomasso himself is described in language which might apply to Juan:

> "Éra grande e bel giovine,—
> Forte, complesso, capel biondo, e un paio
> D'occhi di nobilita pieni e di fuoco;
> Un carattere franco, un umor gaio,
> E colle donne avea sempre un buon giucco."[3]

The scene in which Tomasso has just been especially favored by the Empress and is receiving congratulations from courtiers is paralleled by that in which Juan is being flattered after a warm greeting by Catharine.[4] Another curious coincidence occurs in the efforts of the court physician to cure the apparent debility of Tomasso and Juan.[5] These similarities are striking enough to furnish some probability that Byron was familiar with the plot of *Il Poema Tartaro*, and, consciously or unconsciously, reproduced some of its features in *Don Juan*.

Casti's satire in this poem, as in *Gli Animali Parlanti*, is comprehensive. Like Byron, he ridicules the Russian language,[6] attacks literary fads, criticises customs-duties,[7]

---

[1] *Il Poema Tartaro*, IV., 76.
[2] *Don Juan*, IX., 81. See also *Don Juan*, IX., 80.
[3] *Il Poema Tartaro*, I., 5.
[4] See *Il Poema Tartaro*, IV., 54–55, and *Don Juan*, IX.,.82.
[5] See *Il Poema Tartaro*, V., 32 ff., and *Don Juan*, X., 39.
[6] See *Il Poema Tartaro*, VIII., 85, and *Don Juan*, VII., 14–15.
[7] See *Il Poema Tartaro*, III., 81, and *Don Juan*, III., 20; X., 69.

and enters into a vigorous denunciation of war. In speaking of soldiers who clash in civil strife, he says, with bitter truth:

> "Non è nobil coraggio e valor vero
> Con queste schiere e quello incontro mena,
> Ma l'impunito di ladron mestiero
> Cui legge alcuna, alcun poter non frena."[1]

Byron makes a charge of the same kind in portraying mercenary warriors as,

> "Not fighting for their country or its crown,
> But wishing to be one day brigadiers;
> Also to have the sacking of a town."[2]

The whole of Canto VI in *Il Poema Tartaro* may be compared with Byron's description of the siege of Ismail in *Don Juan*, VII and VIII. Both scenes are presented with grim and graphic realism, without any softening of the horrors and disgusting incidents of warfare.

In *Il Poema Tartaro*, more than in his other productions, Casti ventured to resort to genuine personal satire. He assailed not only Catharine, but also Potemkin, Prince Henry of Prussia, Gustavus III of Sweden, the Sultan of Egypt, and the king of Denmark, to mention only figures who have a prominent place in history. His method being still usually indirect and dramatic, Casti seldom lets himself appear as accuser, but puts criticism of these sovereigns into the mouths of his characters, especially Tomasso's friend, Siveno, who acts as the favorite's mentor and guide. A whole race may arouse Casti's anger—

> "Contro il mogol superbo, e vile
> Mi sento in sen esaltar la bile"—

[1] *Il Poema Tartaro*, VI., 98.,   [2] *Don Juan*, VII., 18.

but he is too wise to let himself be entangled in any contro- versy. This discretion does not, necessarily, imply coward- ice or fear, for his indirect attacks are often as malignant as any of Byron's more direct invectives, and their victims cannot be mistaken. Byron, however, always wished to meet his enemies face to face, while Casti preferred to reach his in a less open way.

In general, the methods employed in *Il Poema Tartaro* are those used in *Gli Animali Parlalti*. There are the same short digressions, illustrated in such passages as,

> "Ciò di Toto piccar dovea la boria
> E con ragion; ma proseguiam la storia,"[1]

in which the author pulls himself away in order to continue his narrative, and which have frequently almost the same phraseology as Byron's "Return we to our story." Some- times the digressions take the form of philosophical reflec- tions on various abstract subjects such as death, mutability, or love:

> "Amor, la bella passion che i petti
> Empie si soavissima dolcezza."[2]

We meet often with the familiar insistence on the veracious character of the author's writing.[3] Irony occurs intermit- tently, mingled at times with sarcasm.

One peculiarity of Casti's manner deserves particular attention, although it is not unique with him and is derived originally from the earlier burlesque poets. This is his habit of shifting the mood from the serious to the ludicrous by the use of unexpected phrases. Examples of this sudden turn in thought are numerous in *Il Poema Tartaro*. When

---

[1] *Il Poema Tartaro*, VIII., 12.   [2] *Ibid.*, III., 68.
[3] *Ibid.*, IV., 69.

the report of rebellion arrives at the Russian court, the
description of terrible alarm ends with the couplet,

"Costernata è la corte epicurea
E venne a Toctabei la diarrea."[1]

The exiled Empress, coming upon her old favorite, Tomasso,
cries,

"Ah, non m'inganno no, quegli è Tomasso
Mel dice il core e lo cognosco al naso."[2]

No reader of *Don Juan* needs to be reminded how often
Byron cuts short a sentimental passage with a remark which
makes the entire situation ridiculous. The secret of this
continual interplay between gravity and absurdity had
never been mastered by Frere; undoubtedly it is one of the
tricks for which Byron was particularly indebted to Casti
and to Casti's predecessors, Pulci and Berni.

Casti's style and language is usually flat and insipid,
undistinguished by beauty or rhythm. "His diction," says
Foscolo, "is without grace or purity." He is often coarse
and unnecessarily obscene. These considerations make it
improbable that Byron could have been affected by Casti's
poetic style, for, despite the sensuousness of some portions
of *Don Juan*, the English poet rarely allowed himself to
sink into the positive indecencies so common in Casti's
work.

On the other hand, the two men are united by their aims
and motives. With all that is petty and offensive in Casti's
satire, there is mingled a real love of liberty and an unswerv-
ing hatred of despotism. No other poet in English or Italian literature of the latter eighteenth and early nineteenth
centuries attempted an indictment of his age, at once so

[1] *Il Poema Tartaro*, VI., 47.   [2] *Ibid.*, XII., 79.

hostile and so comprehensive as those which Casti and Byron tried to make. More significant still, Casti, unlike Pulci, Berni, and Frere, was modern in spirit, and played with vital questions in society and government. He was close to Byron's own epoch, and the objects of his wrath, as far as systems and institutions are concerned, were the objects of Byron's satire. Up to a certain point, too, Byron followed Casti's methods: he is colloquial, discursive, and gossipy; he cares little for plot structure; he employs irony and mockery, as well as invective; and he skips, in a single stanza, from seriousness to absurdity. The differences between the two poets are to be attributed chiefly to the Englishman's genius and powerful personality. He was more of an egotist than Casti, more vehement, more straightforward, more impulsive, and was able to fill *Don Juan* with his individuality as Casti was never able to do with *Gli Animali Parlanti* and *Il Poema Tartaro*.

Certain facts in the relationship between Casti and Byron seem, then, to be clear. At a period before the composition of *Beppo*, Byron had read and enjoyed in the original Italian, the *Novelle* and *Gli Animali Parlanti*. Numerous features in *Beppo* and *Don Juan* which resemble characteristics of Casti's poems had, apparently, existed combined in no English work before Byron's time. In addition, internal evidence makes it a possibility that Byron was familiar with *Il Poema Tartaro*, and that he borrowed from it something of its material and its spirit. The probability is that Byron was influenced, to an extent greater than has been ordinarily supposed, by the example and the methods of Casti.

Byron's acquaintance with Pulci and Berni did not, apparently, begin until after the publication of *Beppo*. On March 25, 1818, hè wrote Murray, in speaking of *Beppo:* "Berni is the original of all—Berni is the father of that kind of writing, which, I think, suits our language, too, very

well."[1]   On February 21, 1820, while he was busy with his
translation of Pulci's *Morgante Maggiore*, he said of Pulci's
poem, to Murray: "It is the parent, not only of *Whistlecraft*, but of all jocose Italian poetry."[2]   These assertions
indicate that Byron classed *Beppo* and *Don Juan* with the
work of the Italian burlesque writers, eventually coming
to recognize Pulci as the founder of the school.

Luigi Pulci (1432–1484), a member of the literary circle
which gathered at the court of Lorenzo de' Medici in the
latter half of the sixteenth century and which included,
among others, Poliziano, Ficino, and Michelangelo, composed the *Morgante Maggiore*, "the first romantic poem of
the Renaissance."   Designed probably to be read or recited
at Lorenzo's table, it was finally completed in February,
1483, as a poem in ottava rima, containing twenty-eight
cantos and some 30,000 lines.[3]   Although the plotting and
consummation of Gan's treason against Charlemagne lends
a crude unity to the romance, it is actually a series of battles, combats, and marvellous adventures loosely strung
together.   The titular hero, Morgante, dies in the twentieth
canto.   The matter is that of the Carolingian legend, now so
well-known in the work of Pulci's successors.

Historically, as the precursor of Berni, Ariosto, and the
other singers of Carolingian romance, Pulci occupies the
position of pioneer.   For our purposes, however, the significance of his work lies less in the incidents of his narrative, the greater part of which he purloined, than in the
poet's personality and the transformation which his grotesque and fanciful genius accomplished with its material.

---

[1] *Letters*, iv., 217.   [2] *Letters*, iv., 407.

[3] In structure, the *Morgante Maggiore*, is made up of the *rifacimenti*
of two earlier works: one, the *Orlando*, rather commonplace and monotonous in tone, was the basis of the first twenty-three cantos; the other,
La Spagna, in prose, loftier and more stately, gave a foundation for the
last five cantos.

Through much humorous and ironic digression, through some amusing interpolated episodes, through a balancing of the serious and the comic elements of the story, through a style popular in origin and humorous in effect, and through the creation of two new characters, the giant Margutte and the demon Astarotte, he made his poem a reflection of his own bourgeois individuality, clever, tolerant, and irrepressible in its inclination to seize upon the burlesque possibilities in men or events.

That the *Morgante Maggiore* is a burlesque poem is due not so much to deliberate design on Pulci's part as to the unconscious reflection of his boisterous, full-blooded, yet at the same time, meditative nature. It is unwise to attribute to him any motive beyond that of amusing his audience. In spite of its apparent irreverence, the *Morgante* was probably not planned as a satire on chivalry or on the church, Pulci—"the lively, affecting, hopeful, charitable, large-hearted Luigi Pulci," as Hunt called him—was at bottom kindly and sympathetic, and his work displays a robust geniality and good-humor which had undoubtedly some influence on *Don Juan*. We rarely find Pulci in a fury; at times his merriment is not far from Rabelaisian, however always without a trace of indignation, for his levity and playfulness seem genuine. This very tolerance is perhaps the product of Renaissance skepticism, which viewed both dogmatism and infidelity with suspicion. Deep emotion, tragedy, and pathos are all to be met with in the *Morgante*, but each is counter-balanced by mockery, comedy, or realism. It is this recurring antithesis, this continual introduction of the grotesque into the midst of what is, by itself, dignified and serious, that is the distinctive peculiarity of Pulci's manner. The mere turn of a phrase makes a situation absurd. There is no intensity about this Florentine; he espouses no theories and advocates no creeds; he is content to have his laugh and to set others chuckling.

This summary may be of service in suggesting one reason why, in the later cantos of *Don Juan*, we sometimes are met with a tolerance almost sympathetic, widely differing from the passionate narrowness of *English Bards*. Pulci, unlike Byron, was not a declared satirist; his theme was in the past, steeped in legend and myth; but something of his spirit, difficult to analyze as that spirit may be, tempered and modified the satire of the older Byron.

Byron's first definite reference to Pulci occurs in a portion of *Don Juan* written in November, 1819:

"Pulci was sire of the half-serious rhyme,
Who sang when chivalry was not Quixotic,
And revelled in the fancies of the time,
True knights, chaste dames, huge giants, Kings despotic."[1]

However, *Don Juan*, III, 45, presenting a possible parallelism with the *Morgante*, XVIII, 115, would indicate that Byron was familiar with Pulci's poem at least some months before.[2] On February 7, 1820, he wrote Murray: "I am translating the first canto of Pulci's *Morgante Maggiore*, and have half done it."[3] In speaking of the completion of the translation, of which he was very proud, he told Murray, February 12, 1820: "You must print it side by side with the original Italian, because I wish the reader to judge of the fidelity; it is stanza for stanza, and often line for line, if not word for word."[4] In the Preface to the translation,

[1] *Don Juan*, IV., 6.
[2] It is probable that Byron had read Merivale's poem, *Orlando in Roncesvalles* (1814), for in the advertisement to his translation of Pulci he refers to "the serious poems on Roncesvalles in the same language [English]—and particularly the excellent one of Mr. Merivale." Merivale's work, based though it is upon the *Morgante*, is without humor, and could have given Byron nothing of the spirit of Pulci.
[3] *Letters*, iv., 402.   [4] *Letters*, iv., 407.

printed with it in *The Liberal*, July 30, 1823, Byron uttered his final word on the Italian writer: "Pulci may be regarded as the precursor and model of Berni altogether . . . He is no less the founder of a' new style of poetry lately sprung up in England. I allude to that of the ingenious Whistlecraft." It is evident, then, that Byron estimated Pulci's work very highly, that he was acquainted, probably, with the entire *Morgante Maggiore* and had studied the first canto, at least, in detail, and that he considered him the original model of Berni and Frere.

It remains to point out specific qualities in manner and style which link the two poets together.[1]   Towards the narrative portion of the *Morgante*, Byron seems to have been indifferent.   In *Don Juan* there is but one clear allusion to the Carolingian legend:

"Just now, enough; but bye and bye I 'll prattle
Like Roland's horn in Roncesvalles' battle."[2]

There is a fairly close parallel already pointed out between the response of a servant to Lambro in *Don Juan*, III, 45, and Margutte's speech in the *Morgante*, XVIII, 115.   There are, however, no other incidents in *Don Juan* which resemble any part of the earlier poem.

Pulci's realism, a quality which is usually in itself burlesque when it is applied to a romantic subject, is shown in his fondness for homely touches and minute details, in his use of words out of the street and proverbs from the lips of the populace.   The interjection of the lower-class spirit into

[1] Cantos III. and IV. of *Don Juan* were written in the winter of 1819–1820, while Byron was at work on his translation of the *Morgante;* hence it is certain that the influence of Pulci may be looked for at least as early as Canto III.   It is probable, moreover, that Byron became acquainted with Pulci's work before, or soon after, the beginning of *Don Juan* in September, 1818.   [2] *Don Juan*, X., 87.

the poem helped to make the *Morgante* in actuality what
Frere had tried to produce in *The Monks, and the Giants*—
a treatment of heroic characters and deeds by a bourgeois
mind. The spectacle of the common vulgar details in the
every-day life of men supposedly great naturally somewhat
degrades the heroes. When Byron portrays General
Suwarrow as

"Hero, buffoon, half-demon, and half-dirt,"[1]

he is following the methods of Pulci, who made his giants
gluttons and his Rinaldo a master of Billingsgate.[2] In
the *Morgante* warriors are continually being put into
ludicrous situations: Morgante fights his battles with a
bell-clapper; Rinaldo knocks a Saracen into a bowl of
soup[3]; and the same noble, turned robber, threatens to steal
from St. Peter and to seize the mantles of St. Ursula and
the Angel Gabriel.[4] Pulci compares Roncesvalles to a pot
in much the same spirit that Byron likens a rainbow to a
black eye.[5] Pulci is fond of cataloguing objects, especially
the varieties of food served at banquets; and Byron shows
the same propensity in describing in detail the viands provided for the feast of Haidée and Juan, and the dinner at
Norman Abbey. Pulci's realism is also manifest in his use
of slang and the language of low life. In this respect, too,
Byron is little behind him: Juan fires his pistol "into one
assailant's pudding"; slang phrases are frequently introduced into *Don Juan*, and elevated poetic style is made more
vivid by contrast with intentionally prosaic passages.

Another peculiarity of Pulci is his tendency to make use
of many Tuscan proverbs and to coin sententious apothegms
of his own. The framework of the octave lends itself easily

[1] *Don Juan*, VII., 55.   [2] *Morgante Maggiore*, XIV., 7.
[3] *Ibid.*, III., 51.   [4] *Ibid.*, XI., 21.
[5] *Don Juan*, II., 92.

to compact maxims in the final couplet, and perhaps it is
due to this fact that *Don Juan* and the *Morgante* are both
crammed with epigrams. In Pulci's poetry one meets on
nearly every page with such apt sayings as

> "La fede è fatta, come fa il solletico"[1]

and

> "Co' santi in chiesa, e co' ghiotti in taverna."[2]

One example out of the many in *Don Juan* will suffice for
quotation:—

> "Adversity is the first path to truth."[3]

Possibly the fact that the *Morgante* was first recited to
the members of Lorenzo's circle is chiefly responsible for
Pulci's habit of turning often to his listeners, inviting them,
as it were, to draw nearer and share his confidence.   Thus
he confesses:

> "Non so se il vero appunto anche si disse;
> Accetta il savio in fin la veria gloria;
> E cosi seguirem la nostra storia."[4]

Byron speaks repeatedly in this sort of mocking apology:

> "If my thunderbolt not always rattles,
> Remember, reader! you have had before,
> The worst of tempests and the best of battles."[5]

Both poets assume, at times, an affected modesty: thus
at the very end of the *Morgante* Pulci asserts that he is not
presumptuous:

[1] *Morgante Maggiore*, XVIII., 117.   [2] *Ibid.*, XVIII., 144.
[3] *Don Juan*, XII., 50.   [4] *Morgante Maggiore*, XXIV., 83.
[5] *Don Juan*, XII., 88.

"Io non domando grillanda d'alloro,
Di che i Greci e i Latini chieggon corona . . .
Anzi non son prosuntuoso tanto,
Quanto quel folle antico citarista
A cui tolse gia Apollo il vivo ammanto; . . .
E cio ch' io penso colla fantasia,
Di piacere ad ognuno e 'l mio disegno."[1]

So Byron refers to his own lack of ambition:

"I perch upon an humbler promontory,
Amidst Life's infinite variety;
With no great care for what is nicknamed Glory."[2]

At the end of nearly every canto of the *Morgante* is a promise
of continuation, so phrased as to seem conventional: *e. g.*,

"Come io diro ne l'altro mio cantare."

The same custom became common with Byron, in such
lines as,

"Let this fifth canto meet with due applause,
The sixth shall have a touch of the sublime."[3]

There is, however, one important distinction between the
two poets in their use of the digression: Pulci employs it for
cursory comment on his story, or for chat about himself;
Byron utilizes it not only for these purposes, but also for
the expression of satire.   It is in his digressions that he
speaks out directly against individuals, institutions, and
society in general.   The *Morgante* is a tale, with an occasional remark by the author; *Don Juan* is a monologue,
sustained by a narrative framework.

Pulci's comparison of his poetry to a boat is introduced

[1] *Morgante Maggiore*, XXVIII., 138–9.   [2] *Don Juan*, XV., 19.
[3] *Ibid.*, V., 159.

so frequently that it may possibly have suggested the figure
to Byron. A typical instance of its usage may be quoted
in the lines:—

> "Io me n'andro con la barchetta mia,
>   Quanto l'acqua comporta un picciol legno."[1]

Byron's employment of the metaphor is also somewhat
frequent:—

> "At the least I have shunned the common shore,
>   And leaving land far out of sight, would skim
>   The Ocean of Eternity: the roar
>   Of breakers has not daunted my slight, trim,
>   But *still* seaworthy skiff; and she may float,
>   Where ships have foundered, as doth many a boat."[2]

It should be added that the brief "grace before meat,"
so apparently truely devotional in phraseology, which Pulci
prefixed to each of his cantos, and the equally orthodox
epilogues in which he gave a benediction to his readers, are
his own peculiarity, borrowed unquestionably from the
street improvisatori. There is nothing corresponding to
them in *Don Juan*.

Both Pulci and Byron were men of wide reading, and not
averse to displaying and making use of their information.
Pulci treats the older poets without reverence: he quotes
Dante's "dopo la dolorosa rotta" without acknowledgment[3];
he burlesques the famous phrase about Aristotle by having
Morgante call Margutte "il mæstro di color che sanno";
and he alludes to Petrarch with a wink:—

---

[1] Other examples occur in the *Morgante Maggiore*, I., 4; II., 1; XIV.,
1; XVI., 1; XXI., 1; XXIV., 1; XXVIII., 1.

[2] *Don Juan*, X., 4.   [3] *Morgante Maggiore*, I., 8.

"O sommo amore, o nuova cortesia!
Vedi che forse ognun si crede ancora,
Che questo verso del Petrarca fa:
Ed e gia tanto, e' lo disse Rinaldo;
Ma chi non ruba è chiamato rubaldo."[1]

This recalls Byron's exhortation at the end of *Don Juan*, I, when, after quoting four lines from Southey, he adds:

"The first four rhymes are Southey's every line:
For God's sake, reader! take them not for mine."

In a similar way Byron gives four lines from Campbell's *Gertrude of Wyoming*, and comments upon them in *Don Juan*, I, 88–89.

This discussion would be incomplete if it did not mention Pulci's fondness for philosophical reflection, meditations on life and death, on joy and sorrow. Volpi has attempted to demonstrate that Pulci, like many so-called humorists, was really, under the mask, a sad man. In making good this thesis he takes such lines as these as indicative of Pulci's true attitude towards the problems of existence:—

"Questa nostra mortal caduca vista
Fasciata ē sempre d'un oscuro velo;
E spesso il vero scambia alla menzogna;
Poi si risveglia, come fa chi sogna."[2]

However this may be, it is certain that Pulci, in his more thoughtful moods, inclined to pessimism and intellectual scepticism.

"Pulci's versification," says Foscolo, "is remarkably fluent; yet he is deficient in melody." Another critic, the author of the brief note in the *Parnaso Italiano*, mentions

[1] *Morgante Maggiore*, XXV., 283.　　　[2] *Ibid.*, XXVIII., 35.

his rapidity and his compression: "Tu troverai pochi poeti, che viaggino so velocemente, come il Pulci, il qualo in otti versi dice spesso piu di otte cose." For this fluency and its corresponding lack of rhythm, the conversational tone of the *Morgante* is largely responsible. The many colloquial digressions and the use of common idioms hinder any approach to a grand style. Pulci's indifference to the strict demands of metre, his employment of abrupt and disconnected phrases, and his frequent sacrifice of melody to vigor and compactness, are also characteristic of Byron's method in his Italian satires. Although *Don Juan* contains some of Byron's most musical passages, it nevertheless gives the impression of having been, like the *Morgante*, composed for an audience, the speaker being, perhaps, governed by rough notes, but tempted from his theme into extemporaneous observations, and caring so little for regularity or unity of structure that he feels no compunction about obeying the inclination of the moment. It is not without some acuteness that he alludes to,

> "Mine irregularity of chime,
>   Which rings what's uppermost of new or hoary,
>   Just as I feel the *Improvvisatore.*"[1]

Specifically in the field of satire, Pulci's work, important though it was in some features of style and manner,[2] exercised its greatest influence on Byron's mood. The chastening effect of Byron's life on his poetic genius had made him peculiarly receptive to the spirit of Pulci's poem;

[1] *Don Juan*, XV., 20.

[2] It is significant that Byron was able to make his translation of the first canto of the *Morgante* so faithful to the original. On September 28, 1820, he wrote Murray:—"The Pulci I am proud of; it is superb; you have no such translation. It is the best thing I ever did in my life" (*Letters*, i., 83). It is obvious that there were features in Pulci's style which appealed to Byron.

and accordingly the Italian poet taught him to take life and
his enemies somewhat less seriously, to be more tolerant
and more genial, to make playfulness and humor join with
vituperation in his satire.   Byron's satiric spirit, through his
contact with Pulci, became more sympathetic, and therefore more universal.

To Berni, whom he, at one time, considered to be the
true master of the Italian burlesque *genre*, Byron has few
references.   We have seen how he was induced to revise his
first opinion and to recognize in Pulci "the precursor and
model of Berni altogether."   In the advertisement to the
translation of the *Morgante* he asserted that Berni, in his
rifacimento, corrected the "harsh style" of Boiardo.   These
meagre data, however, furnish no clue to the possible influence of Berni's work upon *Don Juan*.

Francesco Berni (1496?–1535)[1] is important here chiefly
because of his *rifacimento*, or revision, of Boiardo's *Orlando
Innamorato*.   In accomplishing this task he completely
made over Boiardo's romance by refining the style, polishing
the verse-structure, inserting lengthy digressions of his own
and following a scheme instituted by Ariosto, prefacing
each canto with a sort of essay in verse.   Berni's purpose,
indeed, was to make the *Innamorato* worthy of the *Furioso*.
His version, however, owing probably to the malice of some
enemy, has reached us only in a mutilated form.   As it
stands, nevertheless, it possesses certain features which
distinguish it from the work of Pulci on the one hand and
that of Casti on the other.

The influence which Berni may have had on Byron's

---

[1] Berni was a priest, who became, with Molza, La Casa, Firenzuola,
and Bini, a member of the famous Accademia della Vignajuoli in Rome,
in which circle he was accustomed to recite his humorous poetry. He
died under suspicious circumstances, perhaps poisoned by one of the
Medicean princesses. He was the bitter enemy of Pietro Aretino, the
most scurrilous satirist of the age.

satires comes mainly from two features of the former's work: his introductions to separate cantos, and his admirable style and versification.   It was Berni's habit to soliloquize before beginning his story: thus Canto IX of the *Innamorato* commences with a philosophical disquisition on the unexpected character of most human misfortunes, leading, by a natural step, to the plot itself.   So, in *Don Juan*, only one canto—the second—begins with the tale itself; every other has a preliminary discussion of one sort or another.[1]   It was also Berni's custom to take formal leave of his readers at the end of each canto, and to add a promise of what was to come.[2]   This habit, all but universal with the Italian narrative poets, Byron followed, although his farewell occurs sometimes even before the very last stanza.   A typical example may be quoted:

> "It is time to ease
> This Canto, ere my Muse perceives fatigue.
> The next shall ring a peal to shake all people,
> Like a bob-major from a village steeple."[3]

Berni's style and diction are far superior to Pulci's. Count Giammaria Mazzuchelli, in the edition of Berni in *Classici Italiani*, says of this feature of his work: "La, facilita della rima congiunta alla naturallezza dell' espressione, e la vivacita de' pensieri degli scherzi uniti a singolare coltura nello stile sono in lui si maravigliose, che viene egli considerate come il capo di si fatta poesia, la quale percio ha presa da lui la denominazione, e suol chimarsi Bernesca."

[1] See, *Don Juan*, XII., 1–22, with its discussion of avarice.
[2] See, for example, the *Innamorato*, II., 70:
> "Ma s'io dicesse ogni cosa al presente
> Da dire un' altra volta non aria;
> Pero tornate, e s'attenti starete,
> Sempre piu belle cose sentirete."
[3] *Don Juan*, VII., 85.

He alone of the three Italian burlesque writers considered,
succeeded in creating a masterpiece of literary art.[1]   In
this respect, then, his influence on Byron may have been
salutary.

Henri Beyle (1783–1842), the self-styled M. Stendhal, is
responsible for the theory, since repeated by other critics,
that Byron's Italian satires owe much to the work of the
Venetian dialect poet, Pietro Buratti (1772–1832).   When
Beyle was with Byron in Milan in November, 1816, he
heard Silvio Pellico speak to Byron of Buratti as a charming
poet, who, every six months, by the governor's orders, paid
a visit to the prisons of Venice.   Beyle's account of the
ensuing events runs as follows: "In my opinion, this
conversation with Silvio Pellico gave the tone to Byron's
subsequent poetical career.   He eagerly demanded the
name of the bookseller who sold M. Buratti's works; and
as he was accustomed to the expression of Milanese blunt-
ness, the question excited a hearty laugh at his expense.
He was soon informed that if Buratti wished to pass his
whole life in prison, the appearance of his works in print
would infallibly lead to the gratification of his desires; and
besides, where could a printer be found hardy enough to run
his share of the risk?—The next day, the charming Con-
tessina N. was kind enough to lend her collection to one of
our party.   Byron, who imagined himself an adept in the
language of Dante and Ariosto, was at first rather puzzled
by Buratti's manuscripts.   We read over with him some of
Goldoni's comedies, which enabled him at last to comprehend Buratti's satires.   I persist in thinking, that for the

---

[1] Many characteristics of the *Innamorato*, however, are like those of
the work of Pulci and Casti.   There are the same equivocal allusions
and obscenities, the same pervasive skepticism and pessimism, and the
same colloquial style that are to be met with in the *Morgante* and the
Novelle.   Berni was perhaps greater as a craftsman and artist, but otherwise had the virtues and the faults of the other burlesque poets.

composition of *Beppo*, and subsequently of *Don Juan*, Byron was indebted to the reading of Buratti's poetry."[1]

A statement so plain by a man of Beyle's authority deserves some attention. The first question which arises in connection with his assertion is naturally, what work Buratti had done before 1817, when Byron began the composition of *Beppo*.[2] After a dissipated boyhood, Buratti had become a member of the *Corte dei Busoni*, a pseudo-Academy which devoted its attention chiefly to satire. Although he was the author of several early lampoons, his first political satire was recited in 1813 among a party of friends at the home of Counsellor Galvagna in Venice. It is, in substance, a lamentation over the fate of Venice, with invective directed against the French army of occupation; Malamani styles it "a masterpiece of subtle sarcasm." Eventually, through the treachery of apparent friends, the verses came to French ears, and Buratti was imprisoned for thirty days, his punishment, however, being somewhat lightened by powerful patrons. Shortly after this episode, he circulated some quatrains of a scurrilous nature on Filippo Scolari, a pedantic youth who had criticised contemporary literary men in a supercilious way. For these insults, Scolari tried to have Buratti apprehended again, but the latter, although he was forced to sign an agreement to write no more satires, received only a reprimand. During this period he had also directed several pasquinades at an eccentric priest, Don Domenico Marienis, who seems to have been a general object of ridicule in Venice.

Such, according to Malamani, was the extent of Buratti's work up to 1816. His masterpiece, the *Storia dell' Elefante*,

---

[1] *Letters*, iii., 444–445.

[2] Buratti's career is treated at length in Vittorio Malamani's monograph, *Il Principe dei satirici Veneziani* (1887). An edition of his poetry, in two volumes, was printed in 1864.

was not written until 1819, too late to have been a strong influence even on *Don Juan*. Of this early satiric verse, no one important poem was composed in ottava rima. The poems, all short and of no especial value as literature, used the Venetian dialect, as far removed from pure Tuscan as Scotch is from English. Their most noticeable characteristic is their prevailing irony, a method of satire of which Byron only occasionally availed himself. With these facts in mind, and with the additional knowledge that Byron was unquestionably influenced by the burlesque writers, it is improbable that Beyle's theory deserves any credence. Beyle has made it clear that Byron, at one time, read Buratti's work with interest; but he has failed to show how the English poet could have acquired anything, either in matter or in style, from the Italian satirist.[1]

Of other Italian poems sometimes mentioned as possibly contributing something to *Don Juan*, no one is worth more than a cursory notice. *La Secchia Rapita*, by Tassoni (1565–1635), is a genuine mock-heroic, the model for Boileau's *Lutrin* and, to some extent, for Pope's *Rape of the Lock*. So far as can be ascertained, Byron has no reference either to the author or to his poem; and since *La Secchia Rapita* preserves consistently the grand style, applying it to

---

[1] Buratti's after-life brought him once into relation with Byron. On the birth of a son to Hoppner, the British Consul at Venice, Byron presented the father with a short madrigal:—

> "His father's sense, his mother's grace,
> In him, I hope, will always fit so;
> With—still to keep him in good case—
> The health and appetite of Rizzo."

The Count Rizzo Pattarol, named in the last line, had the verses translated into several languages, in the Italian version changing the word "appetite" to "buonomore." This piece of vanity so excited the mirth of Buratti that he commemorated the affair in an epigram. Byron, however, seems to have paid no attention to the incident.

trivial subjects, it has little in common with Byron's satires.[1]

With *Il Ricciardetto*, by Forteguerri (1675–1735), Byron was better acquainted. Indeed Foscolo, without giving proof for his conclusion, suggested that it might have offered some ideas to the English writer. The Italian poem, completed about 1715, after having been composed, according to tradition, at the rate of a canto a day, contains thirty cantos in ottava rima. It is an avowed burlesque, in which heroes of Carolingian romance are degraded to buffoons, Rinaldo becoming a cook and Ricciardetto a barber. In it, as Foffano says, "the marvellous becomes absurd, the sublime, grotesque, and the heroic, ridiculous." Forteguerri's design, however, was not directly satiric, and he was seldom a destructive critic. His mission was solely to divert his readers. Byron refers to Lord Glenbervie's rendering of the first canto of *Il Ricciardetto* (1822) as most amusing,[2] but he seems to have had no great interest in the original.

A point has now been reached where it is practicable to frame some generalizations as to the extent and nature

---

[1] There is less of the mock-heroic in *Don Juan* than is ordinarily supposed. It has little in common with the classical Mock-Epic, represented in English by the *Dunciad*, the *Scribleriad*, and the *Dispensary*, poems which use the epic machinery of gods and goddesses, ridiculing the manner of the Greek and Roman epics through the method of parody. *Don Juan*, on the other hand, is unrelated to the work of either Homer or Virgil. Nor does it burlesque the Italian epics: its characters, modern and unconventional as they are, are not, even in a humorous sense, heroic, and the matter dealt with is borrowed from none of the Italian romances. The fact that exalted emotions are made absurd, or that fine feelings are jeered at does not warrant us in classing *Don Juan* with the mock-heroic poems. Indeed, the mere absence of the typical addresses to the Muse—they occur only twice in *Don Juan* (II., 7; III., 1)—indicates that Byron did not imitate the epic form.

[2] *Letters*, vi., 50.

of Byron's indebtedness to the Italians. For his subject-matter, he owed them something. The Catharine II episode in *Don Juan* may have been suggested by *Il Poema Tartaro;* an occasional unimportant incident or situation may have been taken or modified from the work of Casti or Pulci. On the whole, however, Byron's material was either original or drawn from other sources than the Italians. Even though Byron and Casti so frequently satirize the same institutions and theories, it is improbable that this is more than coincidence, the result of the natural opposition which similar abuses aroused in men so alike in temperament and intellect.

In his manner, however, Byron was profoundly affected, so much so that his own statement about *Beppo*—"The style is not English, it is Italian"—[1] is in exact accordance with the impression which *Beppo*, as well as *Don Juan*, makes on the reader. He learned, in part from Casti, and later from Berni and Pulci, the use of the burlesque method; he adopted their discursive style, with its opportunities for digression and self-assertion, and made it a channel for voicing his own beliefs as well as for speaking out against his enemies. Accepting the hint offered by their tendency to colloquial speech, he lowered the tone of his diction and addressed himself often directly to his readers. Moreover, he acquired the habit of shifting suddenly from seriousness to absurdity, from the pathetic to the grotesque, in the compass of a single stanza. His wrath, at first untempered, was now softened by a new attitude of skepticism which turned him more to irony and mockery than to violent rage.

In utilizing the octave for his own satires, he gave it a freedom of which it had never before been made capable in English; and, by a clever employment of double and triple rhymes, and by the constant use of run-on lines and stanzas,

[1] *Letters*, iv., 217.

he adjusted the measure to the conversational flow of his verse.

At a time, then, when his youthful narrowness was developing into the maturity that comes only from experience, and when, therefore, he was most susceptible to broadening influences, Byron, fortunately for his satire, was brought into contact with the Italian spirit. The result was that *Don Juan* joined many of the most powerful features of *English Bards* with the lighter elements of Berni and Casti.

The beauty of Byron's satire at its finest in *Don Juan* and *The Vision of Judgment*, lies in the welding of the direct and indirect methods, in the interweaving of invective with burlesque, in such a way that the poems seem to link the spirit of Juvenal with the spirit of Pulci. The consequence is a variety of tone, a widening of scope, and a considerable increase in effectiveness. Byron's general attacks are relieved from the charge of futility; his vindictiveness is mitigated by humor and a touch of the ridiculous; and his aggressiveness, though it does not disappear, is sometimes changed to a cynical tolerance.

CHAPTER VIII

"DON JUAN"

WITH the exception of *The Ring and the Book, Don Juan*, containing approximately 16,000 lines, is probably the longest original poem in English since the *Faerie Queene;* moreover, if we exclude the *Canterbury Tales*, no other work in verse in our literature attempts an actual "criticism of life" on so broad a scale. It is Byron's deliberate and exhaustive characterization of his age, the book in which he divulges his opinions with the least reticence and the most finality. With all their occasional brilliance and power, his earlier satires had been essentially imitative and could be judged by pre-existing standards. Later, in composing *Beppo*, Byron discovered that he had found a kind of verse capable of free and varied treatment and therefore especially suited to his improvising and discursive genius; accordingly, in *Don Juan*, which is a longer and more elaborate *Beppo*, he produced a masterpiece which, besides being an adequate revelation of his complex personality, is unique in English, anomalous in its manner and method.[1]

Because it reflects nearly every side of Byron's variable individuality, *Don Juan*, though satirical in main intent, combines satire with many other elements. It is tragic, sensuous, humorous, melancholy, cynical, realistic, and exalted, with words for nearly every emotion and temper.

---

[1] "This poem [*Don Juan*] carries with it at once the stamp of originality and defiance of imitation." (Shelley, Letter to Byron, Oct. 21, 1821).

It contains a romantic story, full of sentiment and tenderness; it rises into passages of lyric and descriptive beauty,
evidently heart-felt; yet these serious and imaginative
details are imbedded in a sub-stratum of satire. Further-
more, its range in substance and style is very great; it
discusses matters in politics, in society, in literature, and in
religion; it shifts in a stanza from grave to gay, from the
commonplace to the sublime.   It is a poem of freedom;
free in thought and free in speech, unrestricted by the
ordinary laws of metre. "The soul of such writing is its
license," wrote Byron to Murray in 1819.

The plot of *Don Juan*, dealing, like the picaresque
romances of Le Sage and Smollett, with a series of adventures in the life of a wandering hero, and interrupted constantly by the comments of the author, has little real unity.
Considered as a satire, however, the poem becomes unified
through the personality behind the stanzas.   It is a colos-
sal monument of egotism; wherever we read, we meet the
inevitable "I."   The poet's interest in the progress of his
characters is so obviously subordinated to his desire for
gossiping with his readers that the plot seems, at times, to be
almost forgotten.   Thus *Don Juan* is as subjective as
Byron's correspondence; indeed ideas were often transferred
directly from his letters to his verses.   There are lines in the
poem which restate, sometimes in the same phraseology,
the confessions and the criticisms recorded by Lady Blessington in her *Conversations with Lord Byron*.   Autobiographical
references are very common, sometimes merely casual,[1]
sometimes used as a text for satire.[2]   The powerful personality of the writer, expressed thus in his work, furnishes it
with a unity which is lacking in the plot.

It is probable that Byron himself had only a vague

---

[1] *Don Juan*, II., 105; II., 166; V., 4; VI., 5-6.
[2] *Ibid.*, V., 33-39.

conception of the structure and limits of his poem. His conflicting assertions, usually half-jocular, concerning his plan or scheme are proof that he cared little about adhering to a closely knit form. He is most to be trusted when he says:

> "Note or text,
> I never know the word which will come next."[1]

or when he confesses to Murray: "You ask me for the plan of Donny Juan: I have no plan—I had no plan; but I had or have materials."[2] The inconsistent statements in the body of the poem are, of course, merely quizzical: thus in the first canto Byron says decidedly,

> "My poem's epic, and is meant to be
> Divided in twelve books";[3]

when the twelfth canto is reached, he has an apology ready:

> "I thought, at setting off, about two dozen
> Cantos would do; but at Apollo's pleading,
> If that my Pegasus should not be foundered,
> I hope to canter gently through a hundred."[4]

As it lengthened *Don Juan* developed more and more into a verse diary, bound, from the looseness of its design, to remain uncompleted at Byron's death.

But whatever may have actuated Byron in beginning *Don Juan* and however uncertain he may have been at first about its ultimate purpose, it soon grew to be primarily satirical. He himself perceived this in describing it to Murray in 1818 as "meant to be a little quietly facetious upon everything"[5] and in characterizing it in 1822 as "a

---

[1] *Don Juan*, IX., 41.   [4] *Don Juan*, XII., 55.
[2] *Letters*, iv., 342.   [3] *Don Juan*, I., 200.   [5] *Letters*, iv., 260.

Satire on *abuses* of the present states of society,"[1] Despite
the intermingling of other elements, the poem is exactly
what Byron called it—an "Epic Satire."[2]   His remark
"I was born for opposition" indicates how much at variance
with his age he felt himself to be; and his inclination to pick
flaws in existing institutions and to indulge in destructive
criticism of his time had become so strong that any poem
which expressed fully his attitude towards life was bound to
be satirical.   Just as the cosmopolitan outlook of the poem
is due partly to Byron's long-continued residence in a
foreign country, so its varied moods, its diverse methods,
and its wide range of subject matter are to be attributed,
to a large extent, to the fact that the composition of *Don
Juan* extended over several years during a period when he
was growing intellectually and responding eagerly to new
ideas.[3]   The work is a fair representation of Byron's
theories and beliefs during the period of his maturity, when
he was developing into an enlightened advocate of progressive and liberal doctrines.   It is an attack on political inertia
and retrogression, on social conventionality, on cant and
sham and intolerance. The intermittent, erratic, and
somewhat imitative radicalism of a few of his earlier poems
has changed into a persistent hostility to all the reactionary
conservation of the time.   *Don Juan* is satiric, then, in that
it is a protest against all that hampers individual freedom
and retards national independence.

The pervasive satiric spirit of *Don Juan* has varied mani-

[1] *Letters*, vi., 155.   [2] *Don Juan*, XIV., 99.
[3] It was begun at Venice, September 6, 1818, and the first two cantos
were published anonymously, July 15, 1819, by Murray.   Despite much
hostile comment, and the reluctance and eventual refusal of Murray to
print the work, Byron continued with his project, entrusting the publication of the poem, after Canto V., to John Hunt.   Canto XVI. was
completed May 6, 1823, and appeared with Canto XV. on March 26,
1824.   Fourteen stanzas of an unfinished Canto XVII. were among his
papers at the time of his death.

festations. In a few passages there are examples of rancor and spite, of direct personal denunciation and furious invective, that recall the satire of *English Bards*. The attacks on Castlereagh and Southey, on Brougham and Lady Byron are in deadly earnest, with hardly a touch of mockery. At the same time Byron relies mainly on the more playful and less savage method which he had learned from the Italians and used in *Beppo*. He himself expressed this alteration in mood by saying,

> "Methinks the older that one grows,
> Inclines us more to laugh than scold."[1]

It is noticeable, too, that in *Don Juan* petulant fury is much less conspicuous than philosophic satire. Byron is assailing institutions and theories as well as men and women. To some extent the poem is a medium for satisfying a quarrel or a prejudice; but to a far greater degree it is a summary of testimony hostile to the reactionary early nineteenth century. The poet still prefers, in many cases, to make specific persons responsible for intolerable systems; but he is gradually forsaking petty aims and rising to a far nobler position as a critic of his age.

The satire in *Don Juan* is still more remarkable when we consider the field which it surveys. Byron is no longer dealing with local topics, but with subjects of momentous interest to all humanity. He is assailing, not a small coterie of editors or an immodest dance, but a bigoted and absolute government, a hypocritical society, and a false idealism, wherever they exist. More than this, he so succeeds in uniting his satire, through the force of his personality, with the eternal elements of realism and romance, that the combination, complex and intricate though it is, seems to represent an undivided purpose.

[1] *Beppo*, 79.

Perhaps the loftiest note in Byron's protest is struck in dealing with the political situation of his day. Despite his noble birth and his aristocratic tastes, he had become, partly through temperamental inclination, partly through association with Moore and Hunt, a fairly consistent republican, though he took care to make it clear, as Nichol points out, that he was "for the people, not of them." Impatient of restraint on his own actions, he extended his belief in personal liberty until it included the advocacy of any democratic movement. It is to his credit, moreover, that he was no mere closet theorist; in Italy he espoused the cause of freedom in a practical way by abetting and joining the revolutionary *Carbonari;* and he died enrolled in the ranks of the liberators of Greece. In *Don Juan* he declares himself resolutely opposed to tyranny in any form, asserting his hatred of despotism in memorable lines:

> "I will teach, if possible, the stones
>   To rise against earth's tyrants.   Never let it
> Be said that we still truckle unto thrones."[1]

Such doctrine was, of course, not new in Byron's poetry. He had already spoken eloquently and mournfully of the loss of Greek independence[2]; he had prophesied the downfall of monarchs and the triumph of democracy[3]; and he had inserted in *Childe Harold* that vigorous apostrophe to liberty:

> "Yet, Freedom, yet thy banner, torn but flying,
>   Streams like the thunder-storm *against* the wind."[4]

In *Don Juan*, however, Byron is less rhetorical and more direct. In expressing his

[1] *Don Juan*, VIII., 135.
[2] *Childe Harold*, II., 74–76.
[3] *Ode to the French*, 91–104.
[4] *Childe Harold*, IV., 92.

> "Plain sworn downright detestation
> Of every despotism in every nation,"[1]

he does not hesitate to condemn all absolute monarchs; moreover he displays a sincere faith in the ultimate success of popular government:

> "I think I hear a little bird, who sings
> The people by and by will be the stronger."[2]

Such lines as these show a maturity and an earnestness that mark the evolution of Byron's satiric spirit from the hasty petulance of *English Bards* to the humanitarian breadth of his thoughtful manhood. Like "Young Azim" in Moore's *Veiled Prophet of Khorassan*, he is eager to march and command under the banner on which is emblazoned "Freedom to the World."

It is characteristic of Byron's later satire that he applied his theory of liberty to the current problems of British politics by assailing the obnoxious domestic measures instituted by the Tory ministry of Lord Liverpool, by condemning the English foreign policy of acquiescence in the legitimist doctrines of Metternich and the continental powers, and by attacking the characters of the ministers whom he considered responsible for England's position at home and abroad. The England of the time of *Don Juan* was the country which Shelley so graphically pictured in his *Sonnet: England in 1819:*—

> "An old, mad, blind, despised, and dying king, . . .
> Rulers who neither see, nor feel, nor know,
> But leech-like to their fainting country cling,
> Till they drop, blind in blood, without a blow, . . .
> A people starved and stabbed in the untilled field."

[1] *Don Juan*, IX., 24.   [2] *Don Juan*, VIII., 50.

It was a nation exhausted by war, burdened with debt, and seething with discontent. The Luddite outbreaks, the "Manchester Massacre," which so excited the wrath of Shelley, and the "Cato Street Conspiracy" showed the temper of the poor and disaffected classes. Unfortunately the cabinet saw the solution of these difficulties not in reform but in repression, and preferred to put down the uprisings by force rather than to remove their causes. For these conditions Byron blamed Castlereagh, the Foreign Secretary.

Byron had never met Castlereagh and had never suffered a personal injury from him; his rage, therefore, was directed solely at the statesman, not at the man. The Secretary had long been detestable to Irish Whigs like Moore[1] and English radicals like Shelley[2]; it remained for Byron to track him through life with venomous hatred and to pursue him beyond the grave with scathing epigrams. For anything comparable aimed at a man in high position we must go back to Marvell's satires on Charles II and the Duke of York or to the contemporary satire in 1762 on Lord Bute. Byron's Castlereagh has no virtues; the portrait, like Gifford's sketch of Peter Pindar, is all in dark colors. The satire is vehement and personal, without malice and without pity.

[1] Many details of Byron's satire may be traced to corresponding passages in the works of Moore, whose *Fudge Family in Paris* (1818) was familiar to him, and whose *Fables for the Holy Alliance* (1823), many of which were written while the two poets were together in Venice, was dedicated to Byron. Moore denounced Castlereagh as a despot, a bigot, and a time-server, ridiculing him especially for the absurdity of his speeches, which were notorious for their mixed metaphors and poorly chosen phrasing.

[2] Shelley in many short squibs, and particularly in the *Mask of Anarchy* (1819), had assailed the ministry. He had compared Castlereagh and Sidmouth, the Home Secretary, to "two vultures, sick for battle" and "two vipers tangled into one" (*Similes for Two Political Characters of 1819*).

Byron also attacked Wellington, but in manner ironic and scornful, as a leader who had lost all claim to the gratitude of the people by allying himself with their oppressors. For George, who as Regent and King, had done nothing to redeem himself with his subjects, Byron had little but contempt. In satirizing these men, however, Byron was perhaps less effective than Moore, over whose imitations of Castlereagh's orations and "best-wigged Prince in Christendom," people smiled when Byron's tirades seemed too vicious.

Through the method commonly called dramatic, or indirect, Byron assailed English politicians in his portrayal of Lord Henry Amundeville, the statesman who is "always a patriot—and sometimes a placeman," and who is representative of the unemotional, just, yet altogether selfish British minister. The type is drawn with considerable skill and with much less rancor than would have been possible with Byron ten years before. Indeed the satire resembles Dryden's in that it admits of a wide application and is not limited to the individual described.

Nothing in Byron's political creed redounds more to his credit than his persistent opposition to all war except that carried on in the "defence of freedom, country, or of laws." Neglecting the pride and pomp of war, he depicted the Siege of Ismail with ghastly realism, laying emphasis on the blood and carnage of the battle and condemning especially mercenary soldiers, "those butchers in large business." Though this attitude towards warfare was not original with him,[1] Byron spoke out with a firmness and pertinacity that marked him as far ahead of his age.

[1] Young had condemned war in *Satire VII.*, 55–68; Cowper had spoken against it in the *Task*, in the lines:—

"War is a game which, were their subjects wise,
Kings would not play at."

Leigh Hunt and Shelley held exactly Byron's opinions, and expressed them repeatedly.

Though Byron, in *Don Juan*, was almost entirely a destructive critic of the political situation in England and in Europe, his ideas were exceedingly influential. In spite of the fact that he had no definite remedy to offer for intolerable conditions, his daring championship of oppressed peoples affected European thought, not only during his lifetime, but also for years after his death. He was revered in Greece as more than mortal; he was an inspiration for Mazzini and Cavour; he seemed to Lamartine an apostle of liberty. It is probably to his insistence on the rights of the people and to his sweeping indictment of autocratic rule that he owes the greatest part of his international recognition.

Byron's iconoclastic tendencies showed themselves also in his attack on English society, in which he aimed to expose the selfishness, stupidity, and affectation of the small class that represented the aristocratic circle of the nation. In dealing with this subject he knew of what he was speaking, for he had been a member and a close observer of "that Microcosm on stilts yclept the Great World." His picture of this upper class is humorous and ironic, but seldom vehement. In a series of vivid and often brilliant character sketches he delineates the personages that Juan, Ambassador of Russia, meets in London, touching cleverly on their defects and vices, and unveiling the sensuality, jealousy, and deceit which their outward decorum covers. Though the figures are types rather than individuals, they were in many cases suggested by men and women whom Byron knew. Possibly the most effective satire occurs in the description of the gathering at Lady Adeline's country-seat, Norman Abbey, where some thirty-three guests, "the Brahmins of the Ton," meet at a fashionable house party.[1]

---

[1] It is possible that Byron, in his description of this assemblage, was influenced to some extent by T. L. Peacock, the friend of Shelley, who had published *Headlong Hall* (1816) and *Nightmare Abbey* (1818). In these books Peacock had created a sort of prose Comedy of Humors by

For these social parasites and office seekers Byron felt
nothing but contempt. His advice to Juan moving among
them is:

"Be hypocritical, be cautious, be
Not what you *seem*, but always what you *see*."[1]

He describes their life as dull and uninteresting, a gay mas-
querade which palls when all its delights have been tried.
Its prudery conceals scandal, treachery, and lust; its great
vices are hypocrisy and cant—"cant political, cant religious,
cant moral."[2] Indeed the satire of *Don Juan*, from Canto
XI to the point where the poem is broken off, is an attack
on pretence and sham, and a vindication of the free and
natural man. Byron's motive may have been, in part, the
desire for revenge on the circle which had cast him out; but
certainly he was disgusted with the narrowness and conventionality of his London life, and his newly acquired
jesting manner found in it a suitable object for satire.

While Byron's liberalism and democracy were doing
effective service in pointing out flaws in existing political
and social systems, he was still maintaining, not without
many inconsistencies, his old conservative doctrines in
literature, and doggedly insisting on the virtue of his literary
commandments:

"Thou shalt believe in Milton, Dryden, Pope;
Thou shalt not set up Wordsworth, Coleridge, Southey."[3]

While he was being hailed as a leader of the romantic school
of poetry, he was still defending the principles of Pope,
praising the work of Crabbe, Rogers, and Campbell, and

---

forming groups of curious eccentrics, each one obsessed by a single
passion or hobby, and by giving each figure a name suggestive of his
peculiar folly.   [1] *Don Juan*, XI., 86.
[2] *Letters*, v., 542.   [3] *Don Juan*, I., 205.

disapproving of the verses of the members of the Lake School. He dedicated *Don Juan*, in a mocking and condescending fashion, to Southey, and described him in the sketch of the bard "paid to satirise or flatter" who sang to Haidee and Juan the beautiful lyric, *The Isles of Greece*.[1] He ridiculed *The Waggoner* and *Peter Bell*, treating Wordsworth with an hostility which is almost inexplicable in view of Byron's indebtedness in *Childe Harold*, III and IV to the older poet's feeling for nature. Only in minor respects had Byron's position changed; he was more appreciative of Scott and less vindictive towards Jeffrey; and he had found at least one new literary enemy in the poetaster, William Sotheby. In general there was little for him to add to what he had already said in *English Bards*. His otherwise progressive spirit had not extended into the field of literary criticism.

It is not at all surprising that a large portion of *Don Juan* should be devoted to two subjects in which Byron had always been deeply interested—woman and love. Nor is it at all remarkable, in view of his singularly complex and variable nature, that the poem should contain not only the exquisite idyll of Haidée but also line after line of cynical satire on her sex. Though Byron's opinion of women was usually not complimentary, sentiment, and even sentimentality of a certain sort, had a powerful attraction for him. If many of his love affairs were followed and even accompanied by cynicism, it was because the passion in such cases was sensual, and in reaction, he went to the other extreme. The influence of the Guiccioli, however, manifest in his descriptions of Haidée and Aurora Raby, was beneficial to Byron's character, and his ideas of love were somewhat altered through his relations with her. At the same time the conventional assertions of woman's inconstancy and treachery so common in his earlier work recur frequently in *Don Juan*.

[1] *Don Juan*, III., 78–87.

Love, according to Byron's philosophy, can exist only
when it is free and untrammelled.   The poet's too numerous
amours and the general laxity of Italian morals had joined
in exciting in him a prejudice against English puritanism;
while his own unfortunate marital experience had convinced
him that "Love and Marriage rarely can combine."[1]   The
remembrance of his married life and his observation in the
land of his adoption were both instrumental in forming his
conclusion:

> "There 's doubtless something in domestic doings,
>   Which forms, in fact, true love's antithesis."[2]

When marriage, then, is so unalluring, the logical refuge is
an honest friendship with a married lady, "of all connections
the most steady."[3]   When Byron does speak of women
with apparent respect, it is always well to search for irony
behind.   If he says, evidently with emotion:

> "All who have loved, or love, will still allow
>   Life has nought like it.   God is love, they say,
>   And love 's a god,"[4]

he qualifies his ecstacy elsewhere by asserting that Love is
"the very God of evil."[5]   Although he protests that he
loves the sex,[6] he must add that they are deceitful,[7] hypocritical,[8] and fickle.[9]

Nothing in the first two cantos of *Don Juan* was more
offensive to Hobhouse and the "Utican Senate" to which
Murray submitted them than the poorly disguised portrayal
of Lady Byron in the character of Donna Inez.   Though

[1] *Don Juan*, III., 5.
[2] *Ibid.*, III., 8.
[3] *Ibid.*, III., 25.
[4] *Ibid.*, VI., 6.
[5] *Ibid.*, II., 205.
[6] *Ibid.*, VI., 27.
[7] *Ibid.*, I., 178; XI., 36.
[8] *Ibid.*, VI., 14.
[9] *Ibid.*, VI., 2.

Byron explicitly disavowed all intention of satirising his
wife directly, no one familiar with the facts could possibly
have doubted that this lady "whose favorite science was
the mathematical," who opened her husband's trunks and
letters, and tried to prove her loving lord mad, and who
acted under all circumstances like "Morality's prim personification" was intended to represent the former Miss
Milbanke and present Lady Byron.

Doubtless there is something artificial and affected in
much of Byron's cynical comment on women and love; but
if we are inclined to distrust this man of many amours who
delights in flaunting his past before the eyes of his shocked
compatriots, we must remember that there is probably no
conscious insincerity in his words. Byron frequently de-
ludes not only his readers but himself, and his satire on
women, when it is not a kind of bravado, is merely part of
his worldly philosophy.

The philosophical conceptions on which *Don Juan* rests
are, in their general trend, not uncommonly satirical; that
is, they are destructive rather than constructive, skeptical
rather than idealistic, founded on doubt rather than on
faith. It is the object of the poem to overturn tottering
institutions, to upset traditions, and to unveil illusions.
Byron's attitude is that so often taken by a thorough man
of the world who has tasted pleasure to the point of satiety,
and who has arrived at early middle age with his enthusiasms
weakened and his faith sunk in pessimism. This accounts
for much of the realism in the poem. Sometimes the poet,
in the effort to portray things as they are, merely tran-
scribes the prose narratives of others into verse,[1] just as

[1] In Canto II., the entire shipwreck episode is a symposium of
accounts of other wrecks taken from Dalzell's *Shipwrecks and Disasters
at Sea* (1812), *Remarkable Shipwrecks* (1813), Bligh's *A Narrative of the
Mutiny of the Bounty* (1790), and *The Narrative of the Honourable John
Byron* (1768), the last named work being the story of the adventures of

Shakspere borrowed passages from North's *Plutarch* for *Julius Cæsar.* More often he undertakes to detect and reveal the incongruity between actuality and pretence, and to expose weakness and folly under its mask of sham. The realism of this sort closely resembles the more modern work of Zola, attributing as it does even good actions to low motives and degrading deliberately the better impulses of mankind. In Byron's case it seems to be the result partly of a wish to avoid carrying sentiment and romance to excess, partly of a distorted or partial view of life. Whatever romance there is in *Don Juan*—and the amount is not inconsiderable—is invariably followed by a drop into bathos or absurdity. The deservedly famous "Ave Maria,"[1] with its exquisite sentiment and melody, is closed by a stanza harsh and grating, which calls the reader with a shock back to a lower level. This juxtaposition of tenderness and mockery, tending by contrast to accentuate both moods, is highly characteristic of the spirit of the poem. Juan's lament for Donna Julia is interrupted by sea-sickness,[2] and his rhetorical address on London, "Freedom's chosen station," is broken off by "Damn your eyes! your money or your life."[3] Byron never overdoes the emotional element in *Don Juan;* he draws us back continually to the commonplace, and sometimes to the mean and vulgar.[4]

Byron's grandfather. His account of the siege and capture of Ismail in Cantos VII. and VIII. is based, even, in minute details, on Decastelnau's *Essai sur l'histoire ancienne et moderne de la Nouvelle Russie.*

[1] *Don Juan*, III., 101–109. [2] *Ibid.*, II., 17–23.
[3] *Ibid.*, XI., 10.

[4] Byron attributed the unpopularity of *Don Juan* with the ladies, and particularly with the Countess Guiccioli, to the fact that it is the "wish of all women to exalt the *sentiment* of the passions, and to keep up the illusion which is their empire" and that the poem "strips off this illusion, and laughs at that and most other things" (*Letters*, v., 321). It was the opposition of the Countess which induced him to promise to leave off the work at the fifth canto, a pledge which he fortunately disregarded after keeping it for several months.

Byron's materialistic and skeptical habit of mind is often put into phraseology that recalls the "Que sais-je?" of Montaigne. Rhetorical disquisitions on the vanity of human knowledge and of worldly achievement had appeared in *Childe Harold*[1]*;* in *Don Juan* the poet dismisses the great problems of existence with a jest:

> "What is soul, or mind, their birth and growth,
>   Is more than I know—the deuce take them both."[2]

In the words of the British soldier, Johnson, to Juan, we have, perhaps, a summary of the position which Byron himself had reached:

> "There are still many rainbows in your sky,
>   But mine have vanished. All, when Life is new,
>   Commence with feelings warm and prospects high;
>   But Time strips our illusions of their hue,
>   And one by one in turn, some grand mistake
>   Casts off its bright skin yearly like the snake."[3]

As a corollary to this recognition of the futility of human endeavor, the doctrine of mutability, so common in Shelley's poetry, appears frequently in *Don Juan*,[4] ringing in the note of sadness which Byron would have us believe was his underlying mood. Curiously enough, though he cynically classed together "rum and true religion" as calming to the spirit,[5] he was chary of assailing Christian theology or orthodox creeds. He preserved a kind of respect for the Church; and even Dr. Kennedy was obliged to admit that on religious questions Byron was a courteous and fair, as well

---

[1] *Childe Harold*, II., 7.
[2] *Don Juan*, VI., 22. See also I., 215; III., 35.   [3] *Ibid.*, V., 21.
[4] *Ibid.*, XI., 82, 86.   [5] *Ibid.*, II., 34.

as an acute, antagonist. Perhaps the half-faith which led him to say once "The trouble is I do believe" may account for the fact that, at a time when William Hone and other satirists were making the Church of England a target for their wit, *Don Juan* contained no reference to that institution. Byron, then, refused to accept any of the creeds and idealisms of his day. His own position, however, was marked by doubt and vacillation, and he took no positive attitude towards any of the great problems of existence. Experience led him to nothing but uncertainty and indecision, with the result that he became content to destroy, since he was unable to construct.

This is no place for discussing the fundamental morality or immorality of *Don Juan*. The British public of Byron's day, basing their judgment largely upon the voluptuousness of certain love scenes and upon some coarse phrases scattered here and there through the poem, charged him with "brutally outraging all the best feeling of humanity." There can be no doubt that Byron did ignore the ordinary standards of conduct among average people; though he asserted "My object is Morality,"[1] no one knew better than he that he was constantly running counter to the conventional code of behavior. Nor can any one doubt, after a study of his letters to Murray and Moore, that he felt a sardonic glee in acting as an agent of disillusion and pretending to be a very dangerous fellow. This spirit led him to employ profanity in *Don Juan* until his friend Hobhouse protested: "Don't swear again—the third 'damn.'"[2] By assailing many things that his time held sacred, by calling love "selfish in its beginning as its end,"[3] and maintaining that the desire for money is "the only sort of pleasure that requites,"[4] Byron drew upon himself the charge of

[1] *Don Juan*, XII., 86.   [2] *Poetry*, VI., 79.
[3] *Don Juan*, IX., 73.   [4] *Ibid.*, XIII., 100.

immorality. The poem, however, does not attempt to justify debauchery or to defend vicious practices; Byron is attacking not virtue, but false sentiment, false idealism, and false faith. His satiric spirit is engaged in analyzing and exposing the strange contradictions and contrasts in human life, in tearing down what is sham and pretence and fraud. Judged from this standpoint, *Don Juan* is profoundly moral.

Fortunately, in this poem the design of which was to exploit the doctrine of personal freedom, Byron had discovered a medium through which he could make his individuality effective, in which he could speak in the first person, leave off his story when he chose, digress and comment on current events, and voice his every mood and whim. The colloquial tone of the poem strikes the reader at once. He censures himself in a jocular way for letting the tale slip forever through his fingers, and confesses with mock humility,

"If I have any fault, it is digression."[1]

The habit of calling himself back to the narrative becomes almost as much of an idiosyncrasy as Mr. Kipling's "But that is another story."[2]   Obviously Byron's words are really no more than half-apologetic; he knew perfectly well what he was doing and why he was doing it. Without insisting too much on the value of a mathematical estimate it is still safe to say that *Don Juan* is fully half-concerned with that sort of gossipy chat with which Byron's visitors at Venice or Pisa were entertained,[3] and as the poem

[1] *Don Juan*, III., 96.

[2] See *Ibid.*, I., 9; II., 8; III., 110; IV., 113; VI., 57, and numerous other instances.

[3] Only in Canto II. does the story begin at once; every other canto has a preliminary disquisition.   Canto IX., containing eighty-five stanzas, uses forty-one of them before the narrative begins, and of the entire

lengthened, his tendency was to neglect the plot more and more. Indeed the justification for treating *Don Juan* as a satire lies mainly in these side-remarks in which Byron discloses his thoughts and opinions with so little reserve. The digressions in the poem are used principally for two purposes: to satirize directly people, institutions, or theories; to gossip about the writer himself. In either case we may imagine Byron as a monologist, telling us what he has done and what he is going to do, what he has seen and heard, what he thinks on current topics, and illustrating points here and there by a short anecdote or a compact maxim. In such a series of observations, extending as they do over a number of years and written as they were under rapidly shifting conditions, it is uncritical to demand unity. We might as well expect to find a model drama in a diary. The important fact is that we have in these digressions a continuous exposition of Byron's satire during the most important years of his life.

The peculiar features of the octave stanza, with its opportunity for double and triple rhymes and the loose structure of its sestette, made it more suited to Byron's genius than the more compact and less flexible heroic couplet. At the same time the concluding couplet of the octave offered him a chance for brief and epigrammatic expression. In general it may be said that no metrical form lends itself more readily to the colloquial style which Byron preferred than does the octave.

In utilizing this stanza, Byron, accepting the methods of Pulci and Casti, allowed himself the utmost liberties in rhyming and verse-structure. We have already seen that

---

number, forty-six are clearly made up of extraneous material. Of the ninety stanzas in Canto XI., over fifty are occupied with Byron's satire on English society and contemporary events. Canto II. is, of course, filled largely with the shipwreck and the episode of Haidée; but in Canto III., over forty of the entire one hundred and eleven stanzas are discursive, and many others are partly so.

in several youthful poems, and, indeed, in some later ephemeral verses, he had shown a fondness for remarkable rhymes. By the date of *Beppo* he had broken away entirely from the rigidity of the Popean theory of poetry, and had confessed that he enjoyed a freer style of writing:

> "I—take for rhyme, to hook my rambling verse on,
> The first that Walker's lexicon unravels,
> And when I can't find that, I put a worse on,
> Not caring as I ought for critics' cavils."[1]

In *Don Juan* this employment of uncommon rhymes had become a genuine art. Byron once declared to Trelawney that Swift was the greatest master of rhyming in English; but Byron is as superior to Swift as the latter is to Barham and Browning in this respect. Indeed Byron's only rival is Butler, and there are many who would maintain, on good grounds, that Byron as a master of rhyming is greater than the author of *Hudibras*. When we consider the length of *Don Juan*, the constant demand for double and triple rhymes, and the fact that Byron seldom repeated himself, we cannot help marvelling at the linguistic cleverness which enabled him to discover such unheard-of combinations of syllables and words. Some of the most extraordinary have become almost classic,[2] *e.g:*—

> "But—Oh! ye lords of ladies intellectual,
> Inform us truly, have they not hen-pecked you all?"[3]

> "Since in a way that's rather of the oddest, he
> Became divested of his native modesty."[4]

Naturally in securing such a variety of rhymes he was

[1] *Beppo*, 52.
[2] For other rhymes of exceptional peculiarity, see *Don Juan*, I., 102; II., 206; II., 207; V., 5.   [3] *Ibid*, I., 22.   [4] *Ibid*., II., 1.

forced to draw from many sources. Foreign languages proved a rich field, and he obtained from them some striking examples of words similar in sound, sometimes rhyming them with words from the same language, sometimes fitting them to English words and phrases. Some typical specimens are worthy of quotation:

Latin—in medias res, please, ease.[1]
Greek—critic is, poietikes.[2]
French—seat, tête-à-tête, bete.[3]
Italian—plenty, twenty, "mi vien in mente."[4]
Spanish—Lopé, copy.[5]
Russian—Strokenoff, Chokenoff, poke enough.[6]

Byron also resorts to the uses of proper names, borrowed from many tongues:

Dante's—Cervantes.[7]
Hovel is—Mephistophelis.[8]
Tyrian—Presbyterian.[9]
Avail us—Sardanapalus.[10]
Pukes in—Euxine.[11]

It may be added, too, that he was seldom over-accurate or careful in making his rhymes exact. In one instance he rhymes certainty—philosophy—progeny.[12] Most stanzas have either double or triple rhymes, but there are occasional stanzas in which all the rhymes are single.[13]

In *Don Juan* run-on lines are the rule rather than the exception. Certain stanzas are really sentences in which the thought moves straight on, disregarding entirely the ordinary restrictions of versification.[14] In more than one

[1] *Don Juan*, I., 6.   [2] *Ibid.*, III., 111.   [3] *Ibid.*, XIII., 94.
[4] *Ibid.*, I., 62.   [5] *Ibid.*, I., 11.   [6] *Ibid.*, VII., 15.
[7] *Ibid.*, VII., 3.   [8] *Ibid.*, XIII., 8.   [9] *Ibid.*, XV., 91.
[10] *Ibid.*, II., 207.   [11] *Ibid.*, V., 5.
[12] *Ibid.*, XIV., 1.   See also I., 25; I., 67; XVI., 4.
[13] *Ibid.*, I., 154; II., 13, 22, 38.
[14] A characteristic example is *Ibid.*, IX., 34.

case the idea is even carried from one stanza to another
without a pause.[1] In one extraordinary instance a word
is broken at the end of a line and finished at the beginning of
the next,[2] following the example set by the Anti-Jacobin
in Rogero's song in *The Rovers*. Like a public speaker,
Byron at times neglects coherence in order to keep the
thread of his discourse or to digress momentarily without
losing grip on his audience.

Much of the humor of *Don Juan* is due to the varied
employment of many forms of verbal wit: puns, plays upon
words, and odd repetitions and turns of expression. The
puns are not always commendable for their brilliance,
though they serve often to burlesque a serious subject. In
at least one stanza Byron uses a foreign language in pun-
ning.[3] In general it is noticeable that puns become more
common in the later cantos of the poem.[4] There are also
many curious turns of expression, comparable only to some
of the quips of Hood and Praed.[5] Frequently, they are
exceedingly clever in the suddenness with which they shift
the thought and give the reader an unexpected surprise, *e.g.*:

"Lambo presented, and one instant more
    Had stopped this canto and Don Juan's breath."[6]

Repetitions of words or sounds often convey the effect of a
pun, *e.g.*:

"They either missed, or they were never missed,
    And added greatly to the missing list."[7]

The witty line,

[1] *Don Juan*, I., 123–124; V., 8–9; V., 18–19; VIII., 109–110.
[2] *Ibid.*, I., 120.   [3] *Ibid.*, XV., 72.
[4] *Ibid.*, VI., 64; VII., 21; VIII., 30; XIII., 75; XIV., 29, 63; XVI., 60,
94, 98.   [5] *Ibid.*, I., 34; VI., 47; VIII., 32.
[6] *Ibid.*, IV., 42.   [7] *Ibid.*, VII., 27.

"But Tom 's no more—and so no more of Tom,"[1]

is an excellent example of Byron's verbal artistry.

It should be added here, also, that Byron displayed a singular capacity for coining maxims and compressing much worldly wisdom into a compact form. Some of his sayings have so far passed into common speech that they are almost platitudes, *e.g.*:

"There is no sterner moralist than pleasure."[2]

As has been pointed out, this kind of sententious utterance in the form of a proverb or an epigram was very common with the Italian burlesque writers, especially with Pulci.

Something of the universality of Don Juan, of its appeal, not only to particular countries and peoples, but also to the world at large, may be indicated by the number of translations of it which exist.[3] It appeared in French in 1827, in Spanish in 1829, in Swedish in 1838, in German in 1839, in Russian in 1846, in Roumanian in 1847, in Italian in 1853, in Danish in 1854, in Polish in 1863, and in Servian in 1888. Since these first versions appeared, other and more satisfactory ones have been published in most of the countries named. It was chiefly through *Don Juan* that Byron became, what Saintsbury calls him, "the sole master of young Russia, young Italy, young Spain, in poetry." In these days when Byron's defence of the rights of the people is less necessary, when his opposition to despotism would

---

[1] *Don Juan*, XI., 20.

[2] *Ibid.*, III., 6. See also I., 63, 65, 72; II., 172, 179; IX., 15, 59; XIII., 6, 19.

[3] Many imitations and parodies of *Don Juan* were printed during Byron's lifetime, and afterwards; among them were Canto XVII. of *Don Juan*, by One who desires to remain a very great Unknown (1832); *Don Juan Junior*, a Poem, by Byron's Ghost (1839); *A Sequel to Don Juan* (1843); *The Termination of the Sixteenth Canto of Lord Byron's Don Juan* (1864), by Harry W. Wetton.

find few tyrants to oppose, and when his condemnation of war has developed into a widespread movement for universal peace, the powerful impetus which his satire gave to the progress of democracy is likely to be overlooked. His attitude of defiance furnished an illustrious example to struggling nations, and gave them hope of better things.[1]

Within this limited space it has been possible to touch only upon one or two phases of the many which this poem, perhaps the greatest in English since *Paradise Lost*, presents to the reader. /Byron's satire, in assuming a wider scope and a greater breadth of view, in growing out of the insular into the cosmopolitan, has also blended itself with romance and realism, with the lyric, the descriptive, and the epic types of poetry until it has created a new literary form and method suitable only to a great genius. His satiric spirit, in assailing not only individuals, but also institutions, systems, and theories of life, in concerning itself less with literary grudges and personal quarrels than with momentous questions of society, in progressing steadily from the specific to the universal, has undergone a striking evolution. The tone of his satire has become less formal and dignified, and more colloquial, while a more frequent use of irony, burlesque, and verbal wit makes the poem easier and more varied. Byron joins mockery with invective, raillery with contempt, so that *Don Juan*, in retaining certain qualities of

---

[1] Byron's influence upon the literature of the nineteenth century may be studied in Otto Weddigen's treatise *Lord Byron's Einfluss auf die Europaischen Litteraturen der Neuzeit* and in Richard Ackermann's *Lord Byron* (pp. 158–182). Collins numbers among his disciples in Germany, Wilhelm Mueller, Heine, Von Platen, Adalbert Chamisso, Karl Lebrecht, Immermann, and Christian Grabbe; among his French imitators, Lamartine, Hugo, de la Vigne, and de Musset; among his followers in Russia, Poushkin and Lermontoff. To these should be added Giovanni Berchet in Italy, and José de Espronceda in Spain. No other English poet, except Shakspere, has impressed his personality so strongly upon foreign countries.

the old Popean satire, seems to have tempered and qualified the acrimony of *English Bards*. The inevitable result of this development was to make *Don Juan* a reflection of Byron's personality such as no other of his works had been. *Don Juan* is Byron; and in this fact lies the explanation of its strength and weakness.

CHAPTER IX

"THE VISION OF JUDGMENT"

BYRON'S *Vision of Judgment*, printed in the first number of *The Liberal*, October 15, 1820, was the climax of his long quarrel with Southey, the complicated details of which have been related at length by Mr. Prothero in his edition of the *Letters and Journals*.[1] Byron's hostility to Southey was due apparently to several causes, some personal, some political, and some literary. He believed that Southey had spread malicious reports about the alleged immorality of his life in Switzerland with Jane Clermont, Mary Godwin, and Shelley; he considered the laureate to be an apostate from liberalism and a truckler to aristocracy; and he had no patience with his views on poetry and his lack of respect for Pope. The two men were, in fact, fundamentally incompatible in temperament and opinions, Southey being firmly convinced that Byron was a dissipated and dangerous debauchee, while Byron thought Southey a dull, servile, and somewhat hypocritical scribbler.

Since *The Vision of Judgment* was Byron's only attempt at genuine travesty, it may be well to differentiate between the travesty and other kindred forms of satire, all of which are commonly grouped under the generic heading, burlesque. Broadly speaking, a burlesque is any literary production in which there is an absurd incongruity in the adjustment of style to subject matter or subject matter to style, humor

---

[1] *Letters*, vi., 377–399.

being excited by a continual contrast between what is high
and what is low, what is exalted and what is commonplace.[1]
The peculiar effect of burlesque is ordinarily dependent
upon its comparison with some form of literature of a more
serious nature. Of the subdivisions of burlesque, the
parody aims particularly at the humorous imitation of the
style and manner of another work, the original characters
and incidents being displaced by incidents of a more trifling
sort. The parody has been a popular variety of satire, and
examples of it may be discovered in the productions of any
sophisticated or critical age.[2] The travesty, in the narrow
sense of the term, is a humorous imitation of another work,
the subject matter remaining substantially the same, being
made ridiculous, however, by a grotesque treatment and a
less imaginative style. A serious theme is thus deliberately
degraded and debased. The commonest subjects of travesty
have been derived, as one might expect, from mythology or
from the great epic poems. Its popularity, except in
certain limited periods, has never equalled that of the
parody.[3]

Considered simply as a travesty, Byron's *Vision* is

[1] Thus in the *Batrachomyomachia* the elevated manner of epic poetry
is used in depicting a warfare between frogs and mice; while in Voltaire's
La Pucelle, the French national heroine is made to behave like a daugh-
ter of the streets.

[2] Some examples of the parody are *The Splendid Shilling* (1701) by
John Philips (1676–1709); *The Pipe of Tobacco* (1734) by Isaac Hawkins
Browne (1760); *Probationary Odes; Rejected Addresses;* and Swinburne's
Heptalogia.

[3] The travesty flourished especially during the 17th century in the
work of Paul Scarron (1610–1660) and his followers in France, and of
Charles Cotton (1630–1687), John Philips (1631–1706), and Samuel
Butler (1612–1680) in England. During this period Virgil and Ovid
were popular subjects for travesty. Several travesties of Homer were
published in England during the 18th century, one of which, by Bridges,
was read by Byron (*Letters*, v., 166).

remarkable in two respects: first, in that it burlesques a
contemporary poem, while most other travesties ridicule
works of antiquity, or at least of established repute; second,
in that it has an intrinsic merit of its own far surpassing
that of the poem which suggested it. Thus the general
dictum that a travesty is valuable chiefly through the
contrast which it presents to some nobler masterpiece is
contradicted by Byron's satire, which is in itself an artistic
triumph.

Southey's *Vision of Judgment*, of which Byron's *Vision*
is a travesty, was written in the author's function as poet-
laureate shortly after the death of George III. on January
29, 1820. Certainly in many ways it lent itself readily to
burlesque.[1] It was composed in the unrhymed dactyllic
hexameter, a measure in which Southey was even less
successful than Harvey and Sidney had been. It was full
of adulation of a king, who, however much he may have
been distinguished for domestic virtues, was surely, in his
public activities, no suitable subject for encomium. It
was dedicated, moreover, to George IV. in language which
seems to us to-day the grossest flattery[2]. The poem itself,
divided into twelve sections, deals with the appearance of
the old King at the gate of heaven, his judgment and beati-
fication by the angels, and his meeting with the shades of
illustrious dead—English worthies, mighty figures of the
Georgian age, and members of his own family.

Many special features of Southey's poem were disagree-

[1] Charles Lamb said of it that it deserved prosecution far more than
Byron's *Vision;* and Nichol has styled it "the most quaintly preposterous panegyric ever penned."

[2] In his dedication Southey called George IV. "the royal and munifi-
cent patron of science, art, and literature," and praised the monarch's
rule as Regent and King as an epoch remarkable for perfect integrity in
the administration of public affairs and for attempts to "mitigate the
evils incident to our state of society."

able to Byron. It was a vindication and a eulogy of the
existing system of government in England, George III,
whom Byron despised, being described as an ideal sovereign.
Southey had made a contemptuous reference to what he
was pleased to call the watchwords of Faction, "Freedom,
Invaded Rights, Corruption, and War, and Oppression," a
summary which must have been distasteful to a man who
had been raising his voice in resistance to political tyranny.
Southey had also carefully omitted Dryden and Pope from
the list of great writers whom George III met in heaven.
On the whole Southey's poem was pervaded by a tone of
arrogance and self-satisfaction which was exceedingly offensive to Byron.

Byron had begun his travesty on May 7, 1821, and had
sent it to Murray from Ravenna on October 4th.[1] Unconscious of the fact that this satire was in Murray's hands,
Southey meanwhile had published his *Letter to the Courier*,
January 5, 1822, vindictively personal, and containing one
unlucky paragraph: "One word of advice to Lord Byron
before I conclude. When he attacks me again, let it be in
rhyme. For one who has so little command of himself, it
will be a great advantage that his temper should be obliged
to keep tune." When this *Letter* came to Byron's notice,
his anger boiled over; he sent Southey a challenge, which
through the discretion of Kinnaird, was never delivered[2];
and he decided immediately to publish his *Vision*, which he
had almost determined to suppress. Murray, however,
delayed the proof, and on July 3, 1822, Byron, irritated by
this tardiness and enthusiastic over his newly planned
periodical, *The Liberal*, sent a letter by John Hunt,[3] the
proprietor of the magazine, requesting Murray to turn the
satire over to Hunt. In the first number of *The Liberal*,
then, the *Vision* was given the most conspicuous position,
printed, however, without the preface, which Murray, either

[1] *Letters*, v., 387.   [2] *Ibid.*, vi., 10.   [3] *Ibid.*, vi., 93.

ignorantly or unfairly, had withheld from Hunt. A vigorous letter from Byron recovered the preface, which was inserted in a second edition of the periodical.[1]   The consequences of publication somewhat justified Murray's apprehensions. John Hunt was prosecuted by the Constitutional Association, and on July 19, 1824, only three days after Byron's body had been buried in the church of Hucknall Torkard, was convicted, fined one hundred pounds, and compelled to enter into securities for five years. In fairness to Byron, it must be added that he had offered to come to England in order to stand trial in Hunt's stead, and had desisted only when he found that such procedure would not be allowed.[2]

In his *Vision*, Byron had at least four objects for his satire. He wished to ridicule Southey's poem by burlesquing many of its absurd elements; he aimed to proceed more directly against Southey by exposing the weak points in his character and career; he desired to present a true picture of George III, in contrast to Southey's idealized portrait; and he intended to make a general indictment of all illiberal government and particularly of the policy then being pursued by the English Tory party. He seized instinctively upon the weaknesses of the panegyric, and while preserving the general plan and retaining many of the characters, freely mocked at its cant and smug conceit. Through a style purposely grotesque and colloquial, he turned Southey's pompous rhetoric into absurdity; by touches of realism and caricature he made the solemn angels and demons laughable; while, occasionally rising to a loftier tone suggestive of the spirit of *Don Juan*, he reasserted his love of liberty and hatred of despotism.

In executing his project, Byron deliberately neglected a large part of Southey's *Vision* and confined himself almost exclusively to the scene at the trial of the King.   He began

[1] *Letters*, vi., 129.   [2] *Ibid.*, vi., 159.

actually with the situation represented in Section IV of Southey's poem, omitting all the preliminary matter, and ended with Southey's Section V, avoiding entirely the meeting of George with the English worthies. So far as subject matter is concerned, Byron travestied only two of the twelve divisions of the earlier work. He concentrated his attention on the judgment of the King, and then deserted formal travesty in order to introduce his attack on Southey.

It was part of Byron's scheme that angels and demons, serious characters in Southey's poem, should be made the objects of mirth. By a dexterous application of realism, he changed the New Jerusalem of Southey into a very earthly place, where angels now and then sing out of tune and hoarse, and where six angels and twelve saints act as a business-like Board of Clerks. These creatures of the spiritual realm are very substantial beings, not at all immune from mortal infirmities and passions. Saint Peter is a dull somnolent personage who grumbles over the leniency of heaven's Master towards earth's kings, and sweats through his apostolic skin at the appalling sight of Lucifer and demons pursuing the body of George to the very doors of heaven. Satan salutes Michael,

> "as might an old Castilian
> Poor noble meet a mushroom rich civilian,"

and the árchangel, in turn, greets the fallen Lucifer superciliously as "my good old friend." It is probable that in this practice of treating with ridicule those beings who are commonly spoken of with reverence, Byron is imitating Pulci, whose angels and devils are also, in their attributes, more human than divine.

Byron's trial scene, in which Lucifer and Michael dispute for the possession of George III, is an admirable travesty of Southey's representation of the same episode. The glorified

monarch of Southey's *Vision* meets in Byron's satire with
scant courtesy from Lucifer, who acts as attorney for the
prosecution.   Lucifer admits the king's "tame virtues" and
grants that he was a " tool from first to last"; but he charges
him with having "ever warr'd with Freedom and the free,"
with having stained his career with "national and individual
woes," with having resisted Catholic emancipation, and
with having lost a continent to his country.   Wilkes and
Junius, the two shamefaced accusers of Southey's *Vision*,
now act in a different manner.   Wilkes scornfully extends
his forgiveness to the king, and Junius, while reiterating the
truth of his original accusations, refuses to be enlisted as an
incriminating witness.   This section of the satire is splen-
didly managed.   The whole assault on the king tends to
show him as more misguided than criminal.   The lines,

> "A better farmer ne'er brush'd dew from lawn,
> A worse king never left a realm undone!"

create a kind of sympathy for George in that they portray
him as a man placed in a position for which he was manifestly unfitted.

Southey's name is mentioned only once before the 35th
stanza of Byron's poem, but from that point until the conclusion the work deals entirely with him.   These stanzas
constitute what is probably Byron's happiest effort at
personal satire.   For once he did not act in haste, but carefully matured his project, studied its execution, and permitted his first impulsive anger to moderate into scorn.
With due attention to craftsmanship, he surveyed and
annihilated his enemy, laughing at him contemptuously
and making every stroke tell.   It should be observed too
that he chose a method largely indirect and dramatic.   He
did not, as in *English Bards*, merely apply offensive epithets;
rather he placed Southey in a ridiculous situation and made

him the sport of other characters. The satire, is, therefore, exceedingly effective since it allows the victim no chance for a reply.[1] By turning the laugh on Southey, Byron closed the controversy by attaining what is probably the most desirable result of purely personal satire—the making an opponent seem not hateful but absurd.

Byron's poem, however, was something more than a chapter in the satisfaction of a private quarrel. It is also a liberal polemic, assailing not only the whole system of constituted authority in England, but also tyranny and repression wherever they operate. The indictment of George III, which at times approaches sublimity, is in reality directed against the entire reactionary policy of contemporary European statesmen and rulers. The doctrines of the revolutionary Byron, already familiar to us in *Don Juan*, are to be found in the ironic stanzas upon the sumptuous funeral of the king, a passage admired by Goethe; respect for monarchy itself had died out in a nobleman who could say of George's entombment:

> "It seemed the mockery of hell to fold
> The rottenness of eighty years in gold."

With all its broad humor, the satire is aflame with indignation. In this respect the poem performed an important public service. In place of stupid content with things as they were, it offered critical comment on existing conditions, comment somewhat biassed, it is true, but nevertheless in refreshing contrast to the conventional submission of the great majority of the British public.

[1] In the only public retort which Southey undertook, a *Letter to the Courier*, December 8, 1824, he could do little more than make charges of misrepresentation, and repeat his accusation that Byron was one "who played the monster in literature, and aimed his blows at women." Southey unwittingly had engaged with too powerful an antagonist and only his want of a sense of humor kept him from appreciating the fact.

Much of what has already been pointed out with regard
to the sources and inspiration of *Don Juan* may be applied
without alteration to *The Vision of Judgment*, which is, as
Byron told Moore, written "in the Pulci style, which the
fools in England think was invented by Whistlecraft—it is
as old as the hills in Italy."[1]   The *Vision*, being shorter
and more unified, contains few digressions which do not
bear directly upon the plot; but it has the same colloquial
and conversational style, the same occasional rise into true
imaginative poetry with the inevitable following drop into
the commonplace, the same fondness for realism, and the
same broad burlesque.[2]   Hampered as it is by the necessity
of keeping the story well-knit, Byron's personality has ample
opportunity for expression.

It is probable that Byron's description of Saint Peter and
the angels owes much to his reading of Pulci.[3] In at least
one instance there is a palpable imitation.   Saint Peter in
the *Vision*, who was so terrified by the approach of Lucifer
that,

> "He patter'd with his keys at a great rate,
> And sweated through his apostolic skin,"[4]

suffered as did the same saint in the *Morgante Maggiore*
who was weary with the duty of opening the celestial gate
for slaughtered Christians:

[1] *Letters*, v., 385.

[2] The recurrence in the *Vision* of many familiar devices of *Don Juan*
reminds us that the *Vision* marks Byron's resumption of the ottava
rima, which he had left off on December 27, 1820, at the completion of
Don Juan, Canto V., because of the request of the Countess Guiccioli
that he discontinue the work.   In the meantime he turned his attention
to the drama, and *Cain, The Two Foscari*, and *Sardanapalus* were published in December, 1821.   The *Vision* then was his only work in the
octave stanza between December 27, 1820, and June, 1822, when he
began Canto VI. of *Don Juan*.

[3] Byron had finished his translation of the first canto of the *Morgante*
in February, 1820.   [4] *The Vision of Judgment*, 25.

"Credo che molto quel giorno s'affana:
    E converrà ch'egli abbi buono orecchio,
    Tanto gridavan quello anime Osanna
    Ch'eran portate dagli angeli in cielo;
    Sicchè la barba gli sudava e 'l pelo."[1]

In employing the realistic method in depicting the angels,
Byron seems to have caught something of Pulci's grotesque
spirit.

One line of the *Vision*,

"When this old, blind, mad, helpless, weak, poor worm,"

seems to imitate the opening of Shelley's powerful *Sonnet;
England in 1819*, already quoted,

"An old, mad, blind, despised, and dying king."

Professor Courthope has suggested that Byron's *Don
Juan* owes something to the work of Peter Pindar.[2]   The
evidence for the relationship seems, however, to be very
scanty.   Wolcot never employed the octave stanza, nor,
indeed, did he ever show evidences of true poetic power.
The two men were, of course, alike in that they were both
liberals, both avowedly enemies of George III, and both outspoken in their dislikes.   But Byron seldom except in parts of
the *Vision* used the method of broad caricature so characteristic of Pindar.   In the *Vision*, too, occurs the only obvious
reference on Byron's part to Pindar's satire.   He describes
the effect of Southey's dactyls on George III, in the lines:

"The monarch, mute till then, exclaim'd, 'What! What!
    Pye come again?   No more—No more of that.'"[3]

[1] *Morgante Maggiore*, XXVI., 91.
[2] *History of English Poetry*, v., 250.
[3] *The Vision of Judgment*, 92.

The couplet recalls Pindar's delightful imitations of that king's eccentric habit of repeating words and phrases. However, Byron's style in both *Don Juan* and the *Vision* is drawn more from Italian than from English models.

The Vision of Judgment is, if we exclude *Don Juan* as being more than satire, the greatest verse-satire that Byron ever wrote. It is only natural then to compare the poem with other English satires which have high rank in our literature. A practically unanimous critical decision has established Dryden's *Absalom and Achitophel* as occupying the foremost position in English satire before the time of Byron. Unquestionably this work of Dryden's is admirable; it is witty, pointed, and direct, embellished with masterly character sketches and almost faultless in style. It does, however, suffer somewhat from a lack of unity, due primarily to the fact that the narrative element in the poem is subordinate to the description. Byron's *Vision*, on the other hand, has a single plot, which is carefully carried out to a climax and a conclusion. Action joins with invective and description in forming the satire. Thus the two poems, approximately the same length if we consider only Part I of *Absalom and Achitophel*, give a decidedly different impression. Dryden's satire seems a panorama of figures, while Byron's has the coherence and clash of a drama.

Absalom and Achitophel is witty but seldom humorous; while Byron joins caricature and burlesque to wit. The best lines in Dryden's poem, such as:

> "Beggar'd by fools, whom still he found too late;
> He had his jest, and they had his estate,"

excite admiration for the author's cleverness, but rarely arouse a smile; the *Vision*, on the contrary, is full of buffoonery. Dryden's sense of the dignity of the satirist's office did not permit him to lower his style, and he never became familiar with his readers; the very essence of Byron's satire is its colloquial character.

Dryden kept his personality always in the background, while the egotistical Byron could not refrain from letting his individuality lend fire and passion to whatever he wrote. Thus the *Vision*, despite the fact that it is the most cool of Byron's satires, cannot be called calm and restrained. Self-control, the will to subdue and govern his impulses and prejudices, was beyond his reach. Fortunately in the *Vision* he did take time to exercise craftsmanship, but he never attained the polished artistry and firm reserve of his predecessor. Certainly in urbanity, in dignity, and in justice Dryden is the superior, just as he is undoubtedly less imaginative, less varied, and less spirited than Byron.

The two satires are, then, radically different in their methods. One is a masterpiece of the Latin classical satire in English, formal and regular, and using the standard English couplet; the other is our finest example of the Italian style in satire—the mocking, grotesque, colloquial, and humorous manner of Pulci and Casti. Both are effective; but one is inclined to surmise that the purple patches in *Absalom and Achitophel* will outlast the more perfect whole of *The Vision of Judgment*.

The probable results of the publication of a work of such a sensational character had been foreseen by both Murray and Longman. When the first number of *The Liberal* appeared containing not only *The Vision of Judgment* but also three epigrams of Byron's on the death of Castlereagh, it was received by a torrent of hostile criticism from the Tory press. The *Literary Gazette* for October 19, 1822, called Byron's work "heartless and beastly ribaldry," and added on November 2, that Byron had contributed to the *Liberal* "impiety, vulgarity, inhumanity, and heartlessness." The *Courier* for October 26 termed him "an

unsexed Circe, who gems the poisoned cup he offers us."
On the Whig side, in contrast, Hunt's *Examiner* for September 29 spoke of it as "a Satire upon the Laureate, which contains also a true and fearless character of a grossly adulated monarch."

Byron himself described it to Murray as "one of my best things."[1]   Later critical opinion has also tended to rank it very high.   Goethe called the verses on George III "the sublime of hatred."   Swinburne, himself a revolutionist but no partisan of Byron's, exhausts superlatives in commenting on it: "This poem—stands alone, not in Byron's work only, but in the work of the world.   Satire in earlier times had changed her rags for robes; Juvenal had clothed with fire, and Dryden with majesty, that wandering and bastard muse.   Byron gave her wings to fly with, above the reach even of these.   Others have had as much of passion and as much of humor; Dryden had perhaps as much of both combined.   But here, and not elsewhere, a third quality is apparent—the sense of a high and clear imagination.—Above all, the balance of thought and passion is admirable; human indignation and divine irony are alike understood and expressed; the pure and fiery anger of men at the sight of wrong-doing, the tacit inscrutable derision of heaven."   Nichol, in his life of Byron, says:—"Nowhere in so much space, save in some of the prose of Swift, is there in English so much scathing satire."

Two figures in Byron's poem have been made the basis of a shrewd comparison by Henley.   He says: "Byron and Wordsworth are like the Lucifer and Michael of *The Vision of Judgment*.   Byron's was the genius of revolt, as Wordsworth's was the genius of dignified and useful submission; Byron preached the doctrine of private revolution, Wordsworth the dogma of private apotheosis—Byron was the passionate and dauntless 'soldier of a forlorn hope,' Words-

[1] *Letters*, vi., 77.

worth a kind of inspired clergyman." Byron's sympathies in the *Vision*, as in *Cain,* were undoubtedly with Lucifer, the rebel and exile, and his poem will live as a satiric declaration of the duty of active resistance to despotism and oppression.

CHAPTER X

"THE AGE OF BRONZE" AND "THE BLUES"

BYRON'S *Monody on the Death of Sheridan*, written at Diodati on July 17, 1816, and recited in Drury Lane Theatre on September 7, was followed by a period of several years in which he ceased to employ the heroic couplet in poetry of any sort. The reasons for this temporary abandonment of what had been, hitherto, a favorite measure, are not altogether clear, although his action may be ascribed, in part, to his renunciation of things English and to the influence upon him of his study of the Italians. During his residence in Italy, Byron used many metrical forms: the Spenserian stanza, ottava rima, terza rima, blank verse, and other measures in some shorter lyrics and ephemeral verses. Not until *The Age of Bronze*, which he began in December, 1822, did he return to the heroic couplet of *English Bards*.

On January 10, 1823, Byron, then living in Genoa, wrote a letter to Leigh Hunt, in which, among other things, he said: "I have sent to Mrs. S[helley], for the benefit of being copied, a poem of about seven hundred and fifty lines length—*The Age of Bronze*—or *Carmen Seculare et Annus haud Mirabilis*, with this Epigraph—'Impar *Congressus* Achilli'." By way of description, he added: "It is calculated for the reading part of the million, being all on politics, etc., etc., etc., and a review of the day in general,—in my

¹ *Letters*, vi., 160–161.

early *English Bards* style, but a little more stilted, and
somewhat too full of 'epithets of war' and classical and
historical allusions."[1]   The work as revised and completed
contains 18 sections and 778 lines.   Originally destined for
The Liberal, it was eventually published anonymously by
John Hunt, on April 1, 1823.

The Age of Bronze is, then, entirely a political satire,
intended chiefly as a counterblast to the recent stringent
regulations of the reactionary Congress of Verona (1822).
It comprises, however, other material: an introductory
passage on the great departed leaders, Pitt, Fox, and
Bonaparte; frequent digressions treating of the struggles
for constitutional government then taking place in Europe;
and some lines attacking the landed proprietors in England
for their luke-warm opposition to foreign war.   It is, in
nearly every sense, a timely poem, although the note of
"Vanitas Vanitatum" sounded in the early sections gives
the satire a universal application.

For a comprehension of Byron's motives in writing *The
Age of Bronze*, it is necessary to understand something of
the situation in Europe at the time.   Following the numer-
ous insurrections of 1820–22 in Spain, Portugal, Naples,
Greece, and the South American States, the European
powers, guided by the three members of the Holy Alliance,
Russia, Prussia, and Austria, sent delegates to meet at
Verona on October 20, 1822, for a consideration of recent
developments in politics.   The leading figure at the conference was Metternich, the Austrian statesman, although
Francis of Austria, Alexander of Russia, and Frederick
William of Prussia were among the monarchs present.
Montmorenci, representing an ultra-royalist ministry under
Villiele, was there to look after the interests of France;
while England, deprived at the last moment of Castlereagh's
services by his suicide, sent Wellington.   The gathering
finally resolved itself into a conclave for the purpose of

discussing the right of France to interfere in the affairs of Spain, by restoring Ferdinand VII, a member of the House of Bourbon, to the throne of which he had been deprived by the Constitutionalists. Wellington, after protesting against the agreement reached by the other envoys to permit the interference of France, left the Congress,[1] by Canning's instructions, in December. His withdrawal, however, did not affect the ultimate decision of the Congress to stamp out revolt whenever it assailed the precious principle of Legitimacy. War between France and Spain broke out in 1823; Ferdinand VII was replaced upon his tottering throne; and the despotic policy of Metternich triumphed, for a time, over democracy. Canning's only reply was to recognize the independence of the rebellious colonies of Spain, and to assert the belligerency of the Greeks, then fighting for their liberty against the Turks.

It is to the year which saw the work of the Congress of Verona that Byron's secondary title, *Annus haud Mirabilis*, obviously refers. In a striking passage in the beginning of the poem, he pays a tribute to the mighty dead, contrasting, by implication, the leaders of the Congress with the departed heroes: Pitt and Fox, buried side by side in Westminster Abbey; and Napoleon,

"Who born no king, made monarchs draw his car."

The summary which Byron presents of Napoleon's career is full of admiration for the fallen emperor's genius, and of resentment at the indignities which, according to contemporary gossip, he had been compelled to undergo on St. Helena. The man "whose game was empires and whose stakes were thrones" was forced, says the poet, to become the slave of "the paltry gaoler and the prying spy." The passage is both an appreciation and a judgment, wavering, as it does, between sympathy and condemnation for the conqueror who burst the chains of Europe only to renew,

"The very fetters which his arm broke through."

The reference to these giants of the past leads Byron naturally to a glorification of such liberators as Kosciusko, Washington, and Bolivar, and to a joyful heralding of revolutions
in Chili, Spain, and Greece:

> "One common cause makes myriads of one breast,
> Slaves of the east, or helots of the west;
> On Andes' and on Athos' peaks unfurl'd,
> The self-same standard streams o'er either world."

Under the influence of this enthusiasm he prophecies a
liberal outburst which will end in the regeneration of Europe.

Contrasted with the optimism of this aspiring idealism
is Byron's gloom over the deeds of the Congress of Verona.
The measures advocated by this gathering, as we have seen,
were reactionary and autocratic; and Byron's description
of it, tinged with liberal sentiment, is vigorously satirical.
In the conference headed by Metternich, "Power's foremost
parasite," he can see nothing but a body of tyrants,

> "With ponderous malice swaying to and fro,
> And crushing nations with a stupid blow."

Many of the allusions in Byron's sketches of the members
recall the language used by Moore in his *Fables for the Holy
Alliance*.   Moore's views of the situation in Europe agreed
substantially with those of Byron.   Byron's reference to
the "coxcomb czar,"

> "The autocrat of waltzes and of war,"

recalls Moore's mention of that sovereign in *Fable I:*

> "So, on he capered, fearless quite,
> Thinking himself extremely clever,
> And waltzed away with all his might,
> As if the Frost would last forever."

Byron accuses Louis XVIII, who was not present at the Congress, of being a gourmand and a hedonist,

> "A mild Epicurean, form'd at best
> To be a kind host and as good a guest."

The same idea is conveyed in Moore's description of that king as,

> "Sighing out a faint adieu
> To truffles, salmis, toasted cheese."

Especially painful to Byron was the report that Marie Louise (1791–1849), Napoleon's widow, who had been secretly married to her chamberlain, Adam de Neipperg, had attended the Congress, and had become reconciled to her first husband's captors. One section of the satire paints a picture of her leaning on the arm of the Duke of Wellington, "yet red from Waterloo," before her husband's ashes have had time to chill.

The most bitter, and, at the same time, the most just satire in the poem is directed at the English landed gentry:

> "The last to bid the cry of warfare cease,
> The first to make a malady of peace."

The rise in prices due to the long-continued war had fattened the purses of the farmers and land-holders in England, and led them to wish secretly for the continuance of the struggle. Byron attacks severely their grudging assent to proposals of peace, and, in a succession of rhymes on the word "rent," points out the selfishness of their position. The diatribe contains some of Byron's most passionate lines:

> "See these inglorious Cincinnati swarm,
> Farmers of war, dictators of the farm;
> *Their* ploughshare was the sword in hireling hands,

Their fields manured by gore of other lands;
Safe in their barns, these Sabine tillers sent
Their brethren out to battle—why? for rent!"

Although an occasional touch of mockery reminds us of
Don Juan, *The Age of Bronze*, in method, shows a reversion
to the invective manner of *English Bards*.   It can hardly be
said, however, that this later satire is any advance over the
earlier poem.   Its allusions are now unfamiliar to the average reader, and the names once so pregnant with meaning
have faded into dim memories.   Although *The Age of
Bronze* has sagacity and practicality, it lacks unity and
concentration.   Without the vehement sweep of *English
Bards*, it is also too rhetorical and declamatory.   Most
readers, despite the flash of spirit which now and then lights
its pages, have found the satire dull.

The Blues, so little deserving of attention in most respects, is unique among Byron's satires for two reasons: it is
written in the form of a play, and it employs the anapestic
couplet metre, used by Anstey and later by Moore.   Byron's
first reference to it occurs in a letter to Murray from
Ravenna, August 7, 1821: "I send you a thing which I
scratched off lately, a mere buffoonery, to quiz *the Blues*,
in two literary eclogues.   If published, it must be *anonymously*—don't let *my* name out for the present, or I shall
have all the old women in London about my ears, since it
sneers at the solace of their ancient Spinsterstry."[1]   On
September 20, 1821, he calls it a "mere buffoonery, never
meant for publication."[2]   Murray, following his usual
custom with literature which was likely to get him into
trouble, cautiously delayed publication, and the poem was
turned over to John Hunt and printed in *The Liberal*, No.
III (pages 1–24), for April 26, 1823.   It was not attributed

---

[1] *Letters*, v., 338.   [2] *Letters*, v., 369.

to Byron by contemporary critics, most of them giving
Leigh Hunt credit for the authorship.

There is nothing in Byron's letters to explain the immediate motive which led the poet to scribble a work so unworthy of his genius. In his journal kept during his society
life in London there are several references to the "blues,"
and later he made some uncomplimentary allusions to them
in *Beppo* and *Don Juan*. In a sense his efforts to ridicule
them seem to parallel the attacks of Gifford on a coterie
equally harmless and inoffensive.

In form the satire is a closet drama in two acts, each
containing approximately 160 lines. The characters represented are intended, in many instances, for living persons.
Thus, in the first act, which takes place before the door of a
lecture room, Inkel, who is apparently Byron, converses
with Tracy, who may be Moore. Within, Scamp, probably
Hazlitt, is delivering a discourse to a crew of "blues, dandies,
dowagers, and second-hand scribes." Among the subjects
for discussion between the two men is Miss Lilac, a spinster,
and heiress, and a Blue, who is doubtless a caricature of Miss
Milbanke, the later Lady Byron. References to "Rene-
gado's Epic," "Botherby's plays," and "the *Old Girl's
Review*" indicate that Byron has returned to some favorite
subjects for his satire.

The second act is located at the home of Lady Bluebottle,
who resembles closely Lady Holland, the well-known Whig
hostess and one of Byron's friends. Sir Richard Bluebottle,
in a monologue, complains of the crowd of,

"Scribblers, wits, lecturers, white, black, and blue,"

who invade his house and who are provided for at his
expense. In the scene which ensues, Inkel acts as a sort of
interlocutor, with the others as a chorus. Wordsworth, the
"poet of peddlers," is satirized in the old fashion of *English
Bards* as the writer who,

"Singing of peddlers and asses,
Has found out the way to dispense with Parnassus."

Southey is referred to as "Mouthy." Of the other figures, Lady Bluemont is, perhaps, Lady Beaumont, and Miss Diddle, Lydia White, "the fashionable blue-stocking." When the party breaks up, Sir Richard is left exclaiming,

"I wish all these people were damned with my marriage."

On May 6, 1823, Byron finished Canto XVI of *Don Juan*. The fourteen extant stanzas of Canto XVII are dated May 8th. Shortly after he made preparations for his expedition to Greece, and, on July 23, 1823, sailed in the *Hercules*, with Gamba and Trelawney, for Cephalonia. From this time on, his work in poetry practically ceased. He wrote Moore from Missolonghi, March 4, 1824: "I have not been quiet in an Ionian Island but much occupied with business. . . . Neither have I continued *Don Juan*, or any other poem."[1] He devoted himself to drilling Greek troops, holding conferences with leaders, and corresponding with the patriot parties. A fever, brought on by over-exposure, attacked him on April 11th, on the 19th, he died. His remains were brought to England, and buried in the little church of Hucknall Torquard, only a few miles from Newstead Abbey.

[1] *Letters*, vi., 336.

CONCLUSION

Mr. Augustine Birrell, in an illuminating essay on the writings of Pope, brings forward, with reference to satire, a standard of judgment which merits a wider application. "Dr. Johnson," says Mr. Birrell, "is more to my mind as a sheer satirist than Pope, for in satire character tells more than in any other form of verse. We want a personality behind—a strong, gloomy, brooding personality; soured and savage if you will—nay, as sour and savage as you like, but spiteful never." Without subscribing unreservedly to Mr. Birrell's preference of Johnson over Pope, we may still point out that the most conspicuous feature of Byron's satire, as, indeed, of most of his other poetry, is the underlying personality of the author, too powerful and aggressive to be obscured or hidden. There have been satirists who, in assuming to express public opinion, have succeeded in partly or entirely effacing themselves, and who have thus acted in the rôle of judicial censors, self-appointed to the task of voicing the sentiments of a party. In the poetry of the *Anti-Jacobin*, it is by no means easy to detect where the work of one Tory satirist leaves off and that of another begins. So in Dryden's work we are seldom confronted directly by the emotions or partialities of the writer himself; *Absalom and Achitophel* gives the impression of a cool impersonal commentary on certain episodes of history, prejudiced perhaps, but carried on with real or feigned calmness. Byron's satire is of a different sort; we can read scarcely a page without recognizing the potency of the personality that produced it. Just as in *Childe Harold* the hero usually represents Byron himself in some of the phases of his complex individuality; just as the Lara and the Corsair of his verse romances and the Cain and Manfred of his dramas are reflections of the misanthropical, theatrical and skeptical poet; so, in the satires, no matter what method he uses, it is always Byron who criticises and assails.

Most of the characteristics which make up this personality accountable for Byron's satiric spirit have been brought out and discussed in previous chapters. The most important of all, probably, is the haste and impetuosity with which he was accustomed to act. In this respect he may be again contrasted with Dryden, who proceeded to satirize an enemy after due preparation, without apparent agitation or excitement, much as a surgeon performs a necessary operation. Even Pope, sensitive and irritable though he was, did not usually strike when his temper was beyond his control. Byron, on the other hand, was, in most cases, feverish and impulsive; what he thought to be provocation was followed at once by a blow. He did not adopt a position of unmoved superiority, but, both too proud and too impatient to delay, sought instinctively to settle a dispute on the spot. Except in some instances notable because of their rarity Byron seems to have had no understanding of the method of toying with a prospective victim; he planned to close with his opponent, to meet him in a grapple, and to overwhelm him by sheer energy and intrepidity.

This want of restraint had, of course, some favorable results on his satire; the work was indisputably vigorous, effective because of the ungoverned passion which sustained it. At the same time this hasty action was detrimental to Byron's art, and accounts, in part, for the frequent lack of subtlety in his satire. We may be roused temporarily by the fury of the lines; but when, in less enthusiastic moods, we examine the details, we miss the technique and the transforming craftsmanship of the supreme artist. Only in *The Vision of Judgment* did he devote himself to devising means for gaining his end in the most dexterous fashion; and the consequence is that poem is the finest of his satires. In the earlier satires we have Byron, the man, talking out spontaneously, angrily, unguardedly, without second thought or reconsideration, like Churchill, a mighty wielder of the bludgeon but a poor master with the rapier.

Byron's satiric spirit was always combative rather than argumentative or controversial. He preferred to assail men rather than principles. When he disliked an institution or a party, his invariable custom was to select some one as its representative and to proceed to call him to account. It is this desire to war with persons and not with theories that explains his attacks on Castlereagh, whom he never knew, but whom he singled out as the embodiment of England's repressive policy. By nature Byron was much more ready to quarrel with the Foreign Minister as an individual than he was to discuss the prudence and expediency of that statesman's measures.

The characteristics so far mentioned could belong only to a daring and fearless man. Byron never hesitated to avow his ideas, nor did he ever retract his invective except in cases in which he had been convinced that he was unjust. He published the *Lines to a Lady Weeping* under his own name at a time when no one suspected his authorship. For years he satirized European sovereigns without showing the slightest sign of trepidation. He espoused unpopular causes, and often, of his own choice, ran close to danger, when mere silence would have assured him security.

But despite the fact that Byron's hatreds were seldom disguised and that he was, on the whole, open and manly in his satire, there is another side to his nature which cannot be left unnoticed. He was, unfortunately, implicated in certain incidents which leave him under the suspicion of a

kind of treachery towards his friends. His lampoon on
Samuel Rogers, beginning,

> "Nose and chin would shame a knocker;
> Wrinkles that would puzzle Cocker;"

and ending,

> "For his merits, would you know 'em?
> Once he wrote a pretty Poem,"

unpublished during his lifetime, was nevertheless a malicious squib directed at a man who had been one of his
closest companions. There can be no doubt, too, that
Byron's satiric ballad on Hobhouse, "My boy Hobbie, O,"
sent secretly to England, was a true stab in the back,
administered to the man who had been his loyal friend.
Byron, moreover, was not always accurate in his charges.
Like most satirists, he exaggerated to gain his point, and
made claims which the evidence did not justify.   Nor is it
in his favor that he chose to attack his wife in public lampoons, and wrote scurrilous epigrams upon dead statesmen.
   This lack of delicacy aside, however, it must be recognized
that Byron's satire was often exerted in condemning real
evils, and that he performed a definite service to humanity.
More than any other man of his time he insisted on liberty
of speech and action in a period when reactionary politicians were in the ascendant. He combated the perennial
forms of hypocrisy and cant which appear constantly in
England. Neither Dryden nor Pope had been the consistent champion of great causes; but Byron so often employed
his satire for beneficial purposes that, despite the vituperation with which it was greeted by conservatives, it became a
powerful influence for good.
   It may be said, in general, of the substance of Byron's
satires, that he devoted very little attention to the faults and

foibles of mankind, taken as a whole. He was usually moved to satire by some contemporary person, event, or controversy, and his criticism was definite, levelled at some specific abuse or evil. In his youth he showed a disposition to take a lofty moral stand, and to preach against vice; but he was ill-suited to didacticism, and soon forsook it altogether. After 1812, his satire had a very intimate connection with the life around him in politics, society, and literature, and reflected the manners and moods of the age. It is to be noted, too, that Byron was, in theory at least, in opposition to the spirit of his time. His belief in liberal doctrines led him to resist much that seemed safe and solid to those in his own class of life. He was not, in his later days, in sympathy with the situation in Europe; and he died too soon to see his progressive ideas bear fruit in the revolutions of 1830 and the Reform Bill of 1832.

In literature Byron satirized, throughout his career, the representatives of the older romantic school: Wordsworth, Coleridge, and Southey. He did this mainly on the ground that their principles of poetry were subversive of the rules handed down by his avowed masters, Pope and Gifford. In thus defending the name and doctrines of Pope, Byron was consistent during his literary lifetime, although he himself wandered from the path which he persistently asserted to be the only right one. In inveighing against Southey, he was, of course, animated largely by personal spite. For minor poetasters, scribblers who might have been made the puppets of a modern *Dunciad*, Byron had little but silent contempt. In literary satire, then, he presents the strange spectacle of a radical striving desperately to support a losing cause, and that cause a conservative one. Progressive in nearly every other respect, Byron persisted in opposing any attempt to deviate from the standard established by Pope.

Byron's satire on society was partly the result of pique.

He who had been for some time its idol, found himself expelled from English society, and, in retaliation, exposed its absurdities and follies. At the same time it is unquestionable that he furthered a reform in ridiculing the cant and sham of English high life. It was in his last saner days that he wrote the cantos of *Don Juan* which treat of the all-pervasive hypocrisy of fashionable circles, and the satire, even to-day, rings true. It is noticeable that he seldom satirizes fads or fashions, and that he rarely, after 1812, attacks private immorality. His zeal is devoted to unveiling pretence, and to describing this outwardly brilliant gathering as it really is.

Since Byron was a radical and a rebel, his satire was devoted, so far as it concerned itself with political questions, to the glorification of liberty in all its forms, and to the vigorous denunciation of everybody and everything that tended to block or discourage progressive movements. In defence of freedom and in resistance to oppression, his satire found its fullest mission and its amplest justification. When continental Europe of the middle nineteenth century thought of Byron, it pictured him as a nobleman who had assailed tyrannical monarchy, who had aided Italy and Greece in their struggles for independence, and who had been willing to fight for the sake of the principles in which he believed. The words of Byron's political creed have a noble ring: "The king-times are fast finishing. There will be blood shed like water, and tears like mist; but the peoples will conquer in the end. I shall not live to see it, but I foresee it."

The broader philosophical satire on humanity in which he was more and more inclined to indulge as he reached maturity is essentially shallow and cynical. As soon as Byron became indefinite, as soon as he undertook to preach, he grew unsatisfactory, for he had no lesson to teach beyond the pessimism of *Ecclesiastes*.

All these objects for satire afforded Byron an opportunity for expressing some much-needed criticism. The most unworthy sections of his satire are those devoted to mere revenge: the unchivalric lines on Lady Byron and Mrs. Clermont; the violent abuse of Southey and Jeffrey; and the treacherous thrusts at Rogers and Hobhouse. In these passages the satirist descends to the lower level of Churchill and Gifford.

It remains to say a word of Byron's methods, a word merely of recapitulation. Preferring directness always, he was inclined by nature to go straight to his goal, to speak his mind out without pausing to devise subtle or devious plans of attack. Except in his Italian satires his procedure was simple enough: he hurled epithets, made scandalous and scurrilous charges, and thought out offensive comments, writing usually in the first person and meeting his enemies face to face in the good old way of his eighteenth century predecessors. It is, perhaps, unsafe, with *Don Juan* and *The Vision of Judgment* before us, to assert that he was incapable of finesse and cunning; but, for the most part, even in these poems, he was more fond of abuse than he was of innuendo and crafty insinuation. His impetuosity and irrepressible impulsiveness, to which we have had occasion so often to refer, did not allow him to dwell scrupulously on artistic effects.

He had, however, two distinct satiric moods: the one, savage, stern, and merciless; the other, mocking, scornful, and humorous. The one resulted in invective, the other, in ridicule and burlesque. One came to him from Juvenal, Pope, and Gifford; the other he learned from Moore, Frere, and the Italians. Thanks to his versatility, he was successful in using both; but his real genius was shown more in the contemptuous mirth of *The Vision of Judgment* than in the fury of *English Bards*.

Unlike Pope, Byron was no adept at framing pointed

phrases.   The beauty of Pope's satire lies in the single lines, in the details and the finish of an epithet.   Byron's work, on the other hand, should be estimated with regard to the general effect.   Few recall particular lines from the passage on Southey in *The Vision of Judgment;* yet every one remembers the complete caricature of the laureate.   Pope manipulated a delicate and fine stencil; Byron painted on the canvas with broad sweeping strokes.

Byron was the last of the great English satirists in verse, and he has had no imitators who have been able to approach his unique style and manner.   It is a curious fact that his influence after his death on nineteenth-century English satire has been almost negligible.   The causes of this decline in satire since Byron's day are not altogether easy to explain. Perhaps it may be accounted for as accompanying the general lack of interest in poetry of any sort so common to-day. Possibly it may be due to the stringency of the laws against libel, which has resulted in the situation described by Sir George Trevelyan in his *Ladies in Parliament:*

"But now the press has squeamish grown, and thinks
        invective rash:
   And telling hits no longer lurk 'neath asterisk and dash;
   And poets deal in epithets as soft as skeins of silk,
   Nor dream of calling silly lords a curd of ass's milk."

In the twentieth century great political problems are usually fought out in the newspapers or in prose pamphlets; the editorials of our daily journals take the place of satires like *The Age of Bronze.*   Doubtless, too, we have grown somewhat refined in our sensibilities and fastidious in our speech, so that we shrink from the cut-and-slash method in poetry. At any rate our English satire since 1830 has inclined toward raillery and humor, wholly unlike the ardent vindictiveness of the men under the Georges.   The old régime died away with Byron; and in its stead we have had the polished cleverness of Praed, the gentle cynicism of Thackeray, the mild sentimentality of Looker and Dobson. Not until very recently have flashes of the invective spirit appeared in the work of William Watson and Rudyard Kipling. The great issues of the twentieth century have stimulated no powerful English satirist in verse.

BIBLIOGRAPHY

THE standard edition of Byron's *Poetical Works* is that by Ernest Hartley Coleridge in seven volumes (London, 1904), which contains an exhaustive bibliography of the successive editions and translations of different poems. The most complete collection of the *Letters and Journals* is that by Rowland E. Prothero in six volumes (London, 1902). Any study of Byron must be largely based on these comprehensive and scholarly works. A fairly detailed list of critical articles on Byron was compiled by Roden Noel in his *Life of Lord Byron;* this, however, needs to be supplemented and revised in the light of recent investigation.

The following list includes only the more important sources of information for this treatise.

ACKERMANN, R.	*Lord Byron*, Heidelberg, 1901.
Anti-Jacobin, Poetry of the,	edited by Charles Edmonds, London, 1890.
ARMSTRONG, J. L.	*Life of Lord Byron*, London, 1858.
ARNOLD, MATTHEW.	*Byron* (In his *Essays in Criticism*, Second Series, London, 1903).
AUSTIN, ALFRED.	*A Vindication of Lord Byron*, London, 1869.
	Byron and Wordsworth (In his *Bridling of Pegasus*, London, 1910.)

BELL, JOHN.   *Fugitive Poetry*, London, 1790. 18 vols. in 9.

BEYLE, HENRI.   *Lord Byron en Italie* (In his *Racine*, Paris, 1854).

BLEIBTREU, K.   *Byron der Uebermensch, Sein Leben und sein Dichten*, Jena, 1897.

BLESSINGTON, LADY.   *Conversations with Lord Byron*, London, 1834.

BRANDES, G.   *Main Currents in 19th Century Literature*, London, 1905.

BRYDGES, SIR SAMUEL E.   *Letters on the Character and Poetical Genius of Lord Byron*, London, 1824.

An Impartial Portrait of Lord Byron, as a Poet and a Man, Paris, 1825.

BURATTI, P.   *Poesie*, Venezia, 1864. 2 vols.

CASTELAR, E.   *Life of Lord Byron, and Other Sketches*, London, 1875.

CASTI, G. B.   *Gli Animali Parlanti*, Londra, 1803. 2 Tome.

Novelle, Parigi, 1804. 3 volumi.

Il Poema Tartaro, Milano, 1871.

CHASLES, V. E. P.   *Vie et influence de Byron sur son époque* (In his *Études sur l' Angleterre au XIX siècle*, 1850.)

CHESTERTON, G. K.   *The Optimism of Byron* (In his *Twelve Types*, London, 1903.)

CHURCHILL, C.   *Poetical Works*, Boston, 1854. (Ed. by Tooke.)

CLINTON, G. — *Memoirs of the Life and Writings of Lord Byron,* London, 1825.

COLLINS, J. C. — *Studies in Poetry and Criticism,* London, 1905.

COURTHOPE, W. J. — *The Liberal Movement in English Literature,* London, 1885. *A History of English Poetry,* London, 1895–1910. 6 vols.

DALLAS, R. C. — *Recollections of the Life of Lord Byron, 1808-1814,* London, 1824.

EDGCUMBE, R. — *Byron, the Last Phase,* New York, 1909.

EICHLER, A. — *John Hookham Frere: Sein Leben und seine Werke; Sein Einfluss auf Lord Byron,* Wien und Leipsig, 1905.

ELZE, KARL. — *Lord Byron: A Biography,* London, 1872.

ESTEVE. — *Byron et le Romantisme français,* Paris, 1907.

FRERE, J. H. — *Works,* London, 1872. 2 vols.

FUHRMAN. — *Die Belesenheit des jungen Byron.*

GALT, JOHN. — *The Life of Lord Byron,* London, 1830.

GAMBA, P. — *A Narrative of Lord Byron's Last Journey to Greece,* London, 1825.

GIFFORD, W. — The *Baviad* and the *Mæviad,* London, 1797.

GILFILLAN, G. — *A Second Gallery of Literary Portraits,* London, 1850.

GUICCIOLI, COUNTESS. — *Lord Byron jugé par les temoins de sa vie,* Paris, 1868.

HANCOCK, A. E.   *The French Revolution and the English Poets*, New York, 1899.

HANNAY, J.   *Satire and Satirists*, London, 1854.

HAZLITT, W.   *The Spirit of the Age*, London, 1825.

HUNT, L.   *Lord Byron, and Some of his Contemporaries*, London, 1828. 2 vols.

JACK, A. A.   *Poetry and Prose*, London, 1912.

JEAFFRESON, J. C.   *The Real Lord Byron*, Leipsig, 1883. 3 vols.

KENNEDY, JAMES.   *Conversations on Religion, with Lord Byron and Others*, London, 1830.

KOEPPEL, E.   *Lord Byron*, Berlin, 1903.

MEDWIN, T.   *Journal of the Conversations of Lord Byron*, London, 1824.

MOORE, THOMAS.   *Letters and Journals of Lord Byron, with Notices of his Life*, London, 1830.
Memoirs, Journal, and Correspondence, London, 1856. 8 vols.

MORE, P. E.   *The Wholesome Revival of Byron.* (In the *Atlantic.* Vol. 82, December, 1898.)

NICHOL, J.   *Byron*, London, 1908. (Eng. Men of Letters Series.)

PARRY, W.   *The Last Days of Lord Byron*, London, 1825.

POPE, A.   *Poetical Works*, London, 1895. 10 vols.

PREVITE-ORTON, C. W.   *Political Satire in English Poetry*, Cambridge, 1910.

PULCI, L.   *Morgante Maggiore*, Venezia, 1784.

PYRE, J. F. A.   *Byron in our Day*. (In the *Atlantic*, Vol. 99, April, 1907.)

ROEVER.   *Lord Byrons Gedanken ueber Alexander Pope's Dichtkunst*, Hanover, 1886.

STEPHEN, L.   *Byron* (In *Dict. of Nat Biog.*, Vol. viii., pp. 132–155).

SWINBURNE, A. C.   *Essays and Studies*, London, 1875.
Miscellanies, London, 1886.

TRELAWNEY, E. J.   *Recollections of the Last Days of Shelley and Byron*, London, 1858.
Records of Shelley, Byron, and the Author, London, 1878.

TRENT, W. P.   *The Byron Revival*. (In the *Forum*, Vol. 26, October, 1898.)

TUCKER, S. M.   *Verse Satire in England before the Renaissance*, New York, 1906.

WEDDIGEN, O.   *Lord Byrons Einfluss auf die europaischen Litteraturen der Neuzeit*, Hannover, 1884.

INDEX

Ackermann, Richard, 186 (note)
Age of Bronze, The, 4, 6, 8, 53, 202–207.
Anstey, Christopher, 30, 32, 40.
Anti-Jacobin, 30–33, 37, 59, 61, 64, 85

Barrett, E. S., 36, 40
Becher, Rev. J. T., 39, 45, 48
Beppo, 6, 7, 8, 93, 113–127, 129–131, 144, 145, 161, 163, 182
Berni, Francesco, 8, 118 (note), 121 (note), 127, 144, 155–157, 161
Birrell, Augustine, Mr., 103, 209
Blackwood's Magazine, 51
Blessington, Countess of, 115, 164.
Blues, The, 207–209
Bowles, Rev. Samuel, 62–63
Brougham, Lord, 48, 167
Burns, Robert, 29
Butler, Samuel, 11, 16, 122, 182
Butler, Dr., 40–41
Buratti, 157–159
Byron, Lady, 107–110, 175–176
Byron, Lord: place among English satirists, 7; divisions of his satire, 8–9; early satiric verse, 39–47; position in 1798; travels in Spain and Greece, 77; life in London, 94; his political beliefs, 95, 143, 168–172, 204; life in Italy, 115–116; death and burial, 208; influence, 185, 186 (note)

Canning, George, 31, 32, 34, 35, 40, 203, 204
Carlisle, Lord, 43 (note), 66–67
Casti, Giambattista, 8, 117, 118–119, 127–144, 161, 162, 181
Castlereagh, Lord, 102, 170–171
Chesterton, G. K., 14
Childe Harold, 6, 7, 77, 78, 110–111, 122, 136 (note)
Churchill, Charles, 3, 21–22, 25; *Apology Addressed to the Critical Reviewers*, 56–58; *Prophecy of Famine*, 66, 88–89
Clarke, Hewson, 67

DATE